WALKING
by the
WAY

HOMESCHOOLING
IN LIGHT OF ETERNITY

ERICA HUNT

I dedicate this book to my Lord and Savior, Jesus Christ.

He is the King of kings and theLord of lords.

May He receive all the glory!

In Walking By the Way, Erica shares from the unique perspective of being a homeschool graduate and a homeschool mom. She addresses many of the nuances and challenges that the homeschooling journey can bring and holds them up to the truths of God's Word. She brings clarity as she reminds the reader that education truly is discipleship. As believers, we are called to walk out our faith in every aspect of our lives, including education.

This book is a call to homeschooling parents who are on the fence about taking their children home. It's a poignant reminder of our God-given right and responsibility to raise a godly generation!

~ Durenda Wilson
Author of The Unhurried Homeschooler and
Unhurried Grace for a Mom's Heart
The host of Durenda Wilson Podcast
durendawilson.com

This book is such a heartfelt message to home school Moms that is so needed today! I wish I would have had this guidance and encouragement when I first started homeschooling. Every thought, idea, and lesson is based solidly on scripture - just as it should be. Erica will become your new best friend through the pages of this book as she continually points you to God's Word.

~Tina Mauldin
Pastor's wife, Homeschool mom of 20 years and
former school teacher.

Forward

BY: KAREN DEBEUS

In a time when truth is continuously being blurred, it is so refreshing to find a book that speaks to the real truth and to the importance of passing that on to the next generation. There is nothing more important in this age we live in than to teach our children the absolute truths of God's word and how to live those out in an ever-changing culture. It is difficult these days to find an author that doesn't waver on this or water it down, but thankfully Erica Hunt stands firm.

I appreciate Erica's real life and practical views on discipling our children. If we as families and as homeschoolers can unite in this area, imagine the mountains we could move! In a time where people are outwardly focused and placing their measure and success in merits and achievements, we know that true success comes from living a life surrendered at the cross and following Jesus. We recognize that homeschooling for eternity is the goal. Unfortunately, too many homeschoolers are getting caught up in the world's views of success and not God's view, which is why I am so thankful Erica Hunt wrote this book.

Her words will be a blessing and encouragement to all who read them. And being a homeschooled child herself, she knows firsthand the impact of being raised and grounded in the Word of God.

I am confident this book will point others to Jesus and ultimately give glory to God as Erica reminds homeschoolers of their purpose. We need more soothing voices like this in a noisy world that continues to stray from God. Thank you to Erica for this light in a dark world. May we all "walk by the way and homeschool for eternity."

Karen Debeus ~ Simply Living For Him
www.simplylivingforhim.com

Table of Contents

Preface

I gazed out the window as we drove into the little town in upstate New York that we would soon call home. The countryside was beautiful! I was filled with excitement for our new adventure; however, this was already our fifth home so moving to yet another state and leaving behind my friends was difficult. What would our new house look like? Would I make new friends? With so many thoughts running through my seven-year-old mind there was one thing that I did not have to worry about and that was going to a new school, because, unlike most kids back then, I was homeschooled.

When we were young, my mom had no intention of homeschooling us. However, when the time came for me to start Kindergarten we were living in a very rough neighborhood in Rhode Island. She would not even allow my sister and me to play with the neighborhood kids so how could she justify sending me off on a bus to spend all day with them? Homeschooling was still quite unheard of at that time but she had a good friend who had decided to homeschool her daughter so my mom stepped out into the unknown alongside her. I can still remember all the fun my friend and I had learning together that first year! Because homeschooling was very rare, I also remember that during the first few years if we were out during a school day we were constantly questioned about why we were not in school. When my mom would tell them that she was homeschooling us, quite often the response was, "Is that legal??" I am thankful that she was willing to go against the flow and be one of the pioneer homeschoolers.

As the years went by, my sister and I learned so much and remained the best of friends. We are both homeschool graduates (K-12th) and now second-generation homeschoolers. I attribute who I am today not only to the Lord but also to the faithfulness of my mother.

I am blessed to write this book from the perspective of someone who had the privilege of being taught by a mom who followed God's command to diligently teach His words to her children. As we walked by the way, as we sat in our house, when we laid down and when we rose up she was pouring God's word into our hearts and our lives. Our homeschool experience truly centered on the Lord and on His word. I am thankful to be the fruit of her labor of love. I have seen firsthand in my own life how the word of God, spoken often to me in my day to day life from a young age, has encouraged and strengthened me in my walk with the Lord and has been a light unto my path through the trials and dark times. His word has not returned void! Years later, it is still working in my life.

Just a year after graduating I met my husband, Jordan, and it was truly "love at first sight" for both of us. We were engaged in just a few weeks and knowing the Lord had brought us together, we were married a couple months later. Jordan had the interesting experience of attending both public and Christian school as well as being homeschooled. We both knew from the start that we wanted to homeschool our children when the time came but the funny thing is even to this day neither of us remember ever having a conversation about it, we just knew.

That was seventeen years ago. We now live in Ohio, we are more in love than ever and the Lord has blessed us with three precious children. I have the amazing privilege of homeschooling them and by God's grace and strength, I am endeavoring to keep the Lord and His word first in our lives, our home and our homeschool. It is not always easy and like everyone else, we have our struggles, but I have found that when I focus on eternity and what truly matters most everything seems to fall into place. He is faithful!

CHAPTER I

The Call

This calling from God to teach our children is such a blessing. Day in and day out, we, as homeschoolers, have the tremendous responsibility and privilege of pointing our children to Christ and leading them in the way they should go. That is what homeschooling for eternity is all about! It is about reaching their hearts. It is not about recreating public school at home, finding the perfect curriculum or having kids who excel above their peers. Even more than the academics and the extracurricular activities, we need to focus on strengthening their relationship with the Lord. We can use the everyday experiences of life to encourage them and explain to them the truths of God's word.

Homeschooling can be both exciting and humbling at the same time. We will have good days and bad days, we will sometimes feel overwhelmed; however, we know that He who called us is faithful and we can do all things through Christ who strengthens us!

When we look closely at this verse:

And these words which I command you today shall be in your heart. You shall teach them diligently to your children and shall talk of them when you sit in your house, when you walk by the way, when you lie down and when you rise up.
DEUTERONOMY 6:6-7

We see God's command to teach our children is not just about school time, although their education is obviously necessary, schools were not created by God. His design from the beginning was for children to be at home with their families and taught by their own parents. Of course, we realize that this is not always possible, sometimes the best option might be sending your child to Christian, private or even public school but that does not exempt us from diligently teaching them of the Lord and His ways. As we read the book of Proverbs we see the Lord admonishing us to teach and train up our own children, as well as many verses instructing children (often written as "my son" but we know it applies to daughters as well) to follow the words and wisdom of their parents.

> My son, hear the instruction of your father,
> and do not forsake the law of your mother.
> **PROVERBS 1:8**

> My son, keep your father's command,
> and do not forsake the law of your mother.
> Bind them continually upon your heart; tie them around
> your neck. When you roam, they will keep you;
> and when you awake they will speak with you.
> **PROVERBS 6:20-22**

We are the ones God has called to teach our children, not the government. So, if that's the case, why do we try so hard to imitate the public school system? Education does not only take place between the ages of 5-18 nor does it only happen during the hours of 9am-3:30pm. It is a way of life. Our kids are constantly learning and growing and even we as adults are as well. Grade levels were created to make teaching large groups of children easier, but real learning is not tied down to grade levels or ages, it is not kids all the same age doing the same thing. That is not the real world. Instead of trying to recreate a classroom setting at home let's remember that the world is our classroom. Life is learning and the most significant things we can teach our children is God's word and His ways. Those are the only things that have eternal value and as the above verse tells us, they will go with our children throughout their lives to protect them and to be a constant reminder to them.

So if our training has such a strong influence on their lives we should take every chance we get from the time we rise up until the time we lie down to diligently teach our children God's ways, talk of Him, and get His word into their hearts. Not only has the Lord commanded us to do it but it will also change their viewpoint of life and of learning.

One way we can do this is to use scripture when talking to our kids, so that it becomes a natural part of their lives. When situations arise in the course of our day, we can use those opportunities to point them to the Lord and His words. I can say from personal experience that it has been such an incredible blessing throughout my life to know God's word. When trials come into my life or circumstances put me in a place where I am not sure what to do, His word comes pouring into my mind to encourage me and to give me the wisdom and guidance I need. His word brings life! He has used His word to bring life to my hopeless situations. None of those years my mom spent reading the Bible to us, quoting scripture and reminding us to look to Jesus were in vain. My sister and I are both saved, serving the Lord and now homeschooling our own children. Her faithfulness is affecting not only her daughters but also her six grandchildren.

Homeschooling can sometimes get tiring and we wonder if it is worth it, if they are actually hearing what we are saying or learning anything. The days can seem long and the years ahead overwhelming, but let us not grow weary for in due season we shall reap. My mom did not faint and now she is reaping the rewards of her labor. I pray that someday our children will say the same about us; that we continued steadfastly through the good days and the bad and taught them in love. We will not only reap the blessings of those rewards in this life but also in the next...for eternity!

As we go through this book I want to focus on the different aspects of Deuteronomy 6:6-7 and how they apply to our homeschool journey. These two short verses have made an impact on how I view my calling as a homeschool mom. I pray that they will challenge you as well in your own homeschool journey.

CHAPTER II

These Words

> " All scripture is given by inspiration of God, and is profitable for doctrine, for reproof, for correction, for instruction in righteousness, that the man of God may be complete, thoroughly equipped for every good work. "

II TIMOTHY 3:16-17

These words, which I command you today shall be in your heart. You shall diligently teach these words to your children. Talk about these words as you walk by the way, as you sit in your house, when you rise up or when you lie down. All day, every day, all the time teach them these words. I guess the Lord must place a lot of value on these words to instruct us to give them so much of our time!

We know that "these words" refer to God's word, the Bible, which is written by the inspiration of God. Therefore, if God spoke these words we know for certain that every word we read is true because God can not lie.

> ### The entirety of Your word is truth.
> ### PSALMS 119:160

God's word is not only true, but it is also a helpful and powerful means of teaching our children. In our homeschool, the first thing we do each morning is spend time reading the Bible, praying and worshipping the Lord together. Giving God and His word priority in our day shows our children firsthand how important He truly is. We should not only be pointing our kids to Jesus and reading the Bible to them during our specific devotional time but also using His word often as we are teaching. Numerous verses in scripture speak of His word bringing wisdom and instruction. He is the best teacher!

> Oh, how I love Your law! It is my meditation all the day.
> You, through Your commandments, make me wiser
> than my enemies. For they are ever with me. I have more
> understanding than all my teachers, For Your testimonies
> are my meditation. I understand more than the ancients,
> because I keep your precepts.
> **PSALMS 119:97-100**

In every circumstance we may face as we go about our homeschool day, we can find the answers we need in God's word. We can open up the Bible with our children and share with them the words of Almighty God. That is so powerful! He has given us this incredible source for wisdom and guidance. When we read in Ephesians about the armor of God, the Bible is likened to a sword. As we go into battle against the enemy, we will need to have our sword ready. Even Jesus, when tempted by Satan came against his attacks by using the scriptures.

> For the word of God is living and powerful, and sharper
> than any two edged sword!
> **HEBREWS 4:12**

We have this power right at our fingertips, most likely lying on our coffee table or on our bookshelf ready to be opened up and shared with our children at any time. If we have taken the time to study it ourselves then we also have it in our hearts, which will make it that much easier to share it with them when opportunities arise. If someone we love tells us something important, we make a point of paying close attention and putting it to memory. How much more should we value the words of our Lord?

Sadly, we live in a time where there are more Bibles than ever before yet less knowledge of God's word. It is the number one bestselling book but one of the least read. We are living in a famine of the true Word of God. Let us pray for revival to hit our world, touch hearts and bring us back to Him and His word. It can start with our family. The Bible is our most valuable teacher's manual yet how often do we forget or neglect to use this God given resource. God is speaking so many things to us in His word; He has so many riches for our hearts that He is just waiting to reveal to us.

My heart stands in awe of Your word. I rejoice at Your word as one who finds treasure.
PSALM 119:161B-162

The Lord commands us to train up our children in the way they should go and diligently teach them His word. God's word will help them continue to serve Him and even when they are old, they will not depart from it. The verses that they memorize or that we quote to them often are hidden in their hearts forever and will guide them in the decisions they face as they grow up. I still clearly remember verses I memorized almost 30 years ago. Memorizing scripture should be a part of our lives. If our children attend a mid-week program at church, they most likely have Bible verses they are working on memorizing for their class.

In addition to those, we can continue hiding God's words in our hearts and the hearts of our children by memorizing scripture at home together. They can be used as penmanship lessons and then displayed somewhere they will be seen often so that we will read them as we go about our day. Soon they will be put to heart. Having His word in their hearts will keep our kids on the right path and help them to resist temptation. Even at their young ages, my children have shared with me how a verse of scripture has come to their mind when they were making a tough decision and how it helped to guide them to the right choice.

> How can a young man cleanse his way? By taking heed according to Your word. With my whole heart I have sought You; Oh, let me not wander from Your commandments! Your word have I hidden in my heart, that I might not sin against You. Blessed are You O Lord! Teach me Your statutes. With my lips I have declared all the judgments of Your mouth. I have rejoiced in the way of Your testimonies, as much as in all riches. I will meditate on Your precepts, and contemplate all Your ways. I will delight myself in Your statutes; I will not forget Your word.
> PSALM 119:9-16

That is more important than a test score any day! Academic success is wonderful, but it is temporal, only what we do for the Lord is eternal!

God gave us many stories in scripture as examples to show and teach us His ways. He knows that we will all go through trials and hard times, as well as enjoying the blessings of the good times. Through it all, He will be there with us just as He was with Abraham, Moses, David, Job, Esther, Daniel, and the three men in the fiery furnace. He has written down these testimonies of His faithfulness to them so that we can know His character and see His faithfulness throughout history. If He did it then He can do it now because He never changes!

> **For whatever things were written before were written for our learning, that we through the patience and comfort of the scriptures might have hope.**
> **ROMANS 15:4**

> **For I am the Lord, I do not change.**
> **MALACHI 3:6**

When our three children were born, they each received a Bible from their great grandparents. Inside the front cover, they had written this thought provoking quote by John Bunyan, "This book will keep you from sin or sin will keep you from this book." As our children grow and mature we want them to be kept from knowing the ravages of sin. Giving them a firm foundation in His word can be the first step to protecting them.

It's amazing what God's word can do! When our oldest daughter was diagnosed with cancer, a couple months before her second birthday, the Lord used His word to speak to our hearts and give us His peace that passes all understanding. When we have been faced with tough decisions, He has used His word to give us the wisdom we needed. When we didn't know where to turn His word was our guide. It is a trustworthy source of true wisdom and comfort.

> **Your word is a lamp unto my feet and**
> **a light unto my path.**
> **PSALMS 119:105**

As we experience the truths in God's word for ourselves the Bible becomes more and more personal to us. The trials of our lives become our testimonies! The victories of our past give us confidence for the future! As we go about our lives as homeschool moms let us not neglect to share the truths we have learned with our children. I love being able to share what the Lord has done in my life with my children and to talk to them about all the times He has used a passage from His word to speak directly to my heart. I pray that He will help us never overlook speaking and regularly studying His word with our children.

CHAPTER III

Your Heart

> *You shall love the Lord your God
> with all your heart, with all your soul,
> and with all your strength.*

DEUTERONOMY 6:5

We worry about reaching our children's hearts, and rightly so, but what about the condition of our own heart? One thing that strikes me about our verse is that it says, "These words which I command you today shall be in *your* heart!" Us. His word needs to be in *our* hearts! How can we teach God's word to our children if we don't know it ourselves? How can we have His words in our own hearts if we never spend time with Him or study His word? We need to store up His word down deep in our hearts so that as we walk by the way, in the course of our everyday lives, we can teach it diligently to our children. What is in our heart will come out.

Out of the abundance of the heart the mouth speaks.
LUKE 6:45

If we want to know what kind of things are in our hearts, we just need to listen to ourselves speak for a few days and we will get a pretty good idea. I pray that it will be...

Speaking to one another in psalms and hymns and
spiritual songs, singing and making melody in your heart
to the Lord, giving thanks always for all things to God.
EPHESIANS 5:19-20

If not, let's ask the Lord to change that. He's the only one who can! Let's make spending time with the Lord and in His word a priority in our lives. We need to be worshipping the Lord and asking Him to be the one to lead and guide our homeschool. Every day we should take time to read His word so that it becomes a natural part of our lives. Growing up my mom set an example for us to set aside time daily to seek the Lord and to read His word which has carried into my adult life. We may think we are too busy, yet we somehow make time for social media or our favorite TV shows. We will make time for whatever has priority in our lives. Let's make God's word, written directly to us, a priority. What could be more important?

> **Seek ye first the kingdom of God and His righteousness and all these things shall be added unto you.**
> **MATTHEW 6:33**

Homeschooling is a big task and we need all the wisdom and help we can get. We want the Lord to be the One to lead our homeschools. He should be the center of it all and as we seek Him first, all of these other things will be added unto us. If we look to ourselves, things will eventually end up falling apart but when we look to Him, He will always be faithful to give us what we need, when we need it.

> **I can do all things through Christ who strengthens me!**
> **PHILIPPIANS 4:13**

Our days should revolve around Jesus! Talking about Him should come as natural as breathing. He has done so much for us and we can share what He has done with our children so that they can see the power of God firsthand. When they see that

God is moving in our hearts it will give them a hunger for Him in their own lives as well. The Lord has given us our children; He has called us to homeschool, so He will provide us with what we need to succeed through His power.

> **Being confident of this very thing, that He who has begun a good work in you will be faithful to complete it.**
> **PHILIPPIANS 1:6**

Waiting on God is so vital to our relationship with Him! As we wait on Him He will give us His power instead of our own. In our own strength, we will fail but with His strength we will be renewed and ready for the challenges of the day. Our homeschool will thrive when we put God first and our kids will benefit from having a mom who is relying on the Lord for her strength.

> **They that *wait* upon the Lord shall renew their *strength*, they shall mount up with wings as eagles, they shall run and not be weary, they shall walk and not faint.**
> **ISAIAH 40:31**

Waiting on the Lord doesn't always come easy for us. Sometimes our spirit is willing, but our flesh is weak. We want to get up and spend time with Him and in His word before our kids get up and the craziness of our day starts, but yet our bed feels so comfortable or we have other things to do that seem more important, so time slips away, and we start our day without the refreshing we need. I've been there many times but I'm thankful we serve a God who is patient with us. He is always there waiting when we take the time to come to Him.

> **This I recall to my mind, therefore I have hope. Through the Lord's mercies we are not consumed, because His compassions fail not. They are new every morning, great is Your faithfulness.**
> **LAMENTATIONS 3:21-23**

God wants us to wait quietly on Him yet the art of waiting and being still seems long lost to our generation. Years ago, life was a lot slower. Now we live in a society where everything is instant. We are not used to having to wait for anything. We have fast food restaurants, high speed internet and two day shipping when we order online. Stores are full of products advertising how quick they are...things like "1 minute", "instant" "precooked" etc. We are so busy running from one activity to the next that it seems we don't have time to wait for anything and yet how many times does God command us to wait?

> **Rest in the Lord, and *wait* patiently for Him.**
> **PSALM 37:7**

> ***Wait* on the Lord, and keep His way.**
> **PSALM 37:34**

> **My soul, *wait* silently for God alone,**
> **for my expectation is from Him.**
> **PSALM 62:5**

In our society, people aren't used to the quiet anymore either. If we have even a moment with nothing to do, we are so quick to grab our phones. Just look around at the coffee shop, waiting room, park bench or even at a red light. Everywhere we go everyone seems to need constant entertainment. No wonder sitting quietly in the secret place, alone in the stillness with God, can seem so difficult for us. And it is difficult, yes, but not impossible. I know from personal experience that His presence is worth the wait. His still, small voice in the quiet hour is worth my time. My father-in-law often says, "Time spent waiting on God is never wasted."

> **Wait on the Lord, be of good courage, and He shall**
> **strengthen *your heart*; wait, I say, on the Lord.**
> **PSALM 27:14**

CHAPTER IV

Teach them Diligently

*Train up a child in the way he should go,
and when he is old he will not depart from it.*

PROVERBS 22:6

The word diligent means to be hard working and persevering. It also has the meaning of being attentive and showing care in the way something is done. We are to *diligently* teach our children. We should work hard at it, persevere even when it gets tough, be attentive to the needs of our children and instruct them with care and love. As homeschoolers, much of our lives revolve around teaching our children. We spend countless hours researching curriculum choices, lesson planning, grading papers and going on field trips. Many of us gave up our careers to be home with our children because we knew it would be worth the sacrifice. Some of us have children with special needs or health issues, others of us are trying to juggle working and homeschooling at the same time. Regardless of our situations, we all are trying to do what is best for our children because of our deep love for them.

It can be hard to be diligent when life does not go as planned. Our daughter, Ashlynn, is a cancer survivor. She was diagnosed with stage III rhabdomyosarcoma at only twenty one months old and we were blessed to celebrate her thirteenth birthday this year. God has been so good! We are incredibly thankful that she is doing so well but during those extremely difficult years it was sometimes hard to continue to be diligent in teaching and training our girls. At times I was just so tired, both physically and emotionally, that it seemed easier to just get by in life, but I knew that each moment I spent with our precious daughters would have an impact on them for eternity so I pressed on. I continued to raise them for the Lord, pray with them and teach them to the best of their young understanding.

Because our girls were both so little at the time, we hadn't officially started homeschooling but as they grew we often had to homeschool around doctor's appointments and therapies. She has some lasting side effects that are still being treated and although they are much less often now we still have occasional times where we work around her appointments. In addition, up until this summer I was an in home child care provider for over 14 years so that I could bring in money while staying home with our children. Raising other people's children can be hard work, especially when you are trying to homeschool at the same time, but the Lord gave me patience and strength when I needed it. We also clean our church twice a week, a job we are blessed to have, not only because of the financial benefit but also because our children are able to come along and help me. Although they are still a work in progress it has helped to teach them diligence, work ethic and responsibility. I understand some of the challenges that come along with trying to balance life, work and homeschool at the same time. We have taken advantage of naptime to get schoolwork done while the kids I babysat were asleep or taken schoolbooks to work on in the car on the way to doctor's appointments or when heading to go clean. The point is, no matter what our circumstance in life, God has called us to be diligent to the task at hand. We must continue to be diligent to teach our children through it all.

> **Whatever your hand finds to do,**
> **do it with all your might.**
> **ECCLESIASTES 9:10A**

Sometimes in our desire to diligently teach our children it becomes easy for us to focus too much on the temporal aspects of homeschooling instead of the eternal. We are always looking for the next best thing to be sure our children excel academically. The abundance of incredible curriculum options available to homeschoolers today is, to say the least, overwhelming! There are so many that I would love to try but unless we did schoolwork from sun up to sun down there is no way we could use everything that looks good. My purpose in writing this book is not to discuss curriculum choices. (Although I'd love to sit down with you over a cup of hot tea and tell you all about my favorites, what has worked for us and what hasn't...etc) The point is, it is not about which curriculum you use. What works for my family may fail miserably for yours and vice versa. It's about putting God first and letting Him direct our homeschool. Curriculum is helpful but it is not the teacher. Curriculum is not what will cause our homeschool to succeed. It is God! He is the One who has given us our children and He will be there to help us teach them. He can use whatever we have if we will just give it to Him.

God has called *us* to teach our children, not the author of a specific curriculum. So, let's pray that the Lord will show us what He wants for us in our homeschool journey, our curriculum choices, our homes and our family and then let's not stress it. Curriculum makes our job easier, can be helpful in teaching our children information that we may not know or explaining things in different ways, but it is still just a tool. We are the ones teaching. We are in control of how and what we teach and we should never feel like a slave to our curriculum. Curriculum is not our master. God is the one who should be the true master of our homeschool. Our real goal is to bring our children to Christ and into a loving relationship with Him.

To Be Educated

If I learn my ABCs, can read 600 words per minute, and can write with perfect penmanship, but have not been taught how to communicate with the Designer of language, I have not been educated.

If I can deliver an eloquent speech and persuade with my stunning logic, but have not been instructed in God's wisdom, I have not been educated.

If I have read Shakespeare and John Locke and can discuss their writings with keen insight, but have not read the greatest of books-the Bible-and have no knowledge of its personal importance, I have not been educated.

If I have memorized addition facts, multiplication tables, and chemical formulas, but have never been disciplined to hide God's word in my heart, I have not been educated.

If I can explain the law of gravity and Einstein's Theory of Relativity, but have never been instructed in the unchangeable laws of the One who orders our universe, I have not been educated.

If I can classify animals by their family, genus and species, and can write a lengthy scientific paper that wins an award, but have not been introduced to the Maker's purpose for all creation, I have not been educated.

If I can recite the Gettysburg Address and the Preamble to the Constitution, but have not learned about the hand of God in the history of our country, I have not been educated.

If I can play the piano, the violin, six other instruments, and can write music that moves listeners to tears but have not been taught to listen to the Director of the universe and worship Him, I have not been educated.

If I can run cross country races, star in basketball, and do 100 push-ups without stopping, but have never been shown how to bend my spirit to do God's will, I have not been educated.

If I can identify a Picasso, describe the style of DaVinci, and even paint a picture that gains acclaim, but have not learned that all harmony and beauty comes from a relationship with God, I have not been educated.

If I graduate with perfect grades and am accepted at the finest university with a full scholarship, but have not been guided into a career of God's choosing for me, I have not been educated.

If I become a good citizen, voting at each election and fighting for what is moral and right, but have not been told of humanities sinfulness and hopelessness without Christ, I have not been educated.

However, if one day I see the world as God sees it,

and come to know Him, Whom to know is life eternal,
and glorify God by fulfilling His purpose for me, then,
I have been educated.

By, Carolyn Caines

If our children have not accepted Jesus as their Savior then it is vital that we show them not only their sinful condition but the salvation that God freely offers them through the death of His Son. Many kids know all of the facts yet they really don't understand why Jesus had to come and die. They may not realize what Jesus' death has to do with them over 2,000 years later. We need to explain the gospel to them from the beginning. When we see our children acting or speaking unkindly or when we see death, pain and suffering in this world, we can remind them that it is all because of sin. God created a perfect world but man chose to disobey. Because of that disobedience, our world is cursed and we are all born sinners deserving of eternal death.

For all have sinned, and come short of the glory of God.
ROMANS 3:23

For the wages of sin is death, but the gift of God is eternal life through Jesus Christ our Lord.
ROMANS 6:23

But God demonstrates His own love toward us, in that while we were yet sinners, Christ died for us.
ROMANS 5:8

How sad it is to realize our own lost condition yet what a blessing it is to see the how far the Lord went to bring us back to Him. When Adam and Eve sinned, God sacrificed a lamb. Blood was shed to cover their sin and nakedness. That was only a temporary solution but the Lord promised to one-day send a Savior who would cover our sins once and for all. He loved us so much that when we were deserving of death, He sent His only Son to die in our place!

> For God so loved the world that He gave His only begotten Son, that whosoever believes in Him shall not perish but have everlasting life.
> **JOHN 3:16**

Jesus was born a man, lived a sinless life and was then willing to take our punishment upon Himself...but that's not the end of the story, after having defeated sin through His death on the cross, He rose again! Death could not hold Him! He suffered all of that for us. What a loving Savior we have!

> He was wounded for our transgressions, He was bruised for our iniquities, the chastisement for our peace was upon Him, and by His stripes we are healed.
> All we like sheep have gone astray; we have turned, everyone, to his own way; and the Lord has laid on Him the iniquity of us all.
> **ISAIAH 53:5-6**

There is nothing we could ever do to deserve salvation. Many people try to do good works to earn their way to heaven, but the Bible is very clear that it is only by trusting in Jesus and allowing His blood to cover our sin that we can be saved and have eternal life.

> **For by grace you have been saved through faith, and not of yourselves; it is the gift of God, not of works, lest anyone should boast.**
> **EPHESIANS 2:8-9**

We need to explain to our children that Jesus is the only way into heaven. We don't want religion, we want a relationship with our heavenly Father through the blood of His Son. We want the security of knowing we are promised a home in heaven someday.

> **Jesus said, "I am the way, the truth and the life. No one comes to the Father except through Me."**
> **JOHN 14:6**

> **He who has the Son has life; he who does not have the Son of God does not have life. These things I have written to you who believe in the name of the Son of God, that you may know that you have eternal life.**
> **I JOHN 5:12-13A**

The most important thing we can ever teach our children is God's plan of salvation for their lives. It is a tremendous blessing to watch them realize their sinfulness, their need for a Savior and to see them submit their lives to Him. Nothing could be better than that. As they walk this Christian life we must be diligent to teach them His ways so that they will continue on the right path; knowing God has a perfect plan for their lives. When they see themselves in the right perspective, as uniquely created by God for His divine purpose their existence will have true meaning.

For we are His workmanship, created in Christ Jesus for good works, which God prepared beforehand that we should walk in them.
EPHESIANS 2:10

There is a verse in scripture that refers to our children as arrows in the hand of a warrior.

Like arrows in the hand of a warrior,
so are the children of one's youth.
PSALM 127:4

We are warriors in a battle for the hearts of our children. Which direction are we aiming our arrows? What is our final target? Are we near sighted, aiming them for a college scholarship, a good career or success in this world- or are we aiming higher than that, looking beyond this world and aiming them towards their eternal home? If we are raising them with their unending future in mind then when the day comes that we must let go of the string and let our arrows fly on their own, we will watch with delight as they soar forward, confident in their faith. Then someday we will spend eternity rejoicing together that we made it to our journey's end.

We need to *diligently* teach our children because we aren't the only ones in this battle trying to influence their lives. The world is constantly trying to lure our children in through music, TV shows, friendships etc. While they are still at home, we can guide them in making the right choices in those areas. Corrie Ten Boom is quoted as saying, "If we don't teach our children to follow Christ, the world will teach them not to." How true that is! The devil is not just sitting back hoping our kids will follow him. He is trying his hardest to destroy their faith.

> **Your adversary the devil walks about as a roaring lion,**
> **seeking whom he may devour.**
> **Resist him steadfastly in the faith.**
> **I PETER 5:8**

If we know that the enemy is working overtime to destroy our kids' faith, then shouldn't we be doing everything we can to resist him? Shouldn't we build up our children's faith? Shouldn't we encourage them to spend time drawing near to God on their own? The closer they walk with God the further away from the world's ways they will be living. His voice will go before them and lead them in the way they should go. His word will be their guidebook for life. We need to teach them God's words so that when Satan comes against them they will be able to resist his temptations.

**Submit to God. Resist the devil, and he will flee from you.
Draw near to God and He will draw near to you.
JAMES 4:7-8**

Let's keep in mind what really matters, and that is our children's hearts and their relationship with the Lord. What has the Lord commanded us to *diligently* teach to our children?... His words! If they learn to read at three yet never read God's word, what profit is it? If they learn everything there is to know about science but don't know the One who created it all we have not been successful in our calling. Certain things may seem important now, but will they matter in 10,000 years? I am in no way suggesting we throw out all other learning and only teach the Bible. That would be ridiculous. We need the Lord to be first and foremost in our homeschool, while not leaving their education undone. Our children need to learn how to write, to read well and how to do mathematics to live in this world. However, we must also remember that we are not of this world. This world is not our home! All those things, although important for us to teach, are not the most important. Our children's souls are what will matter for eternity. Our life on this Earth is like a vapor but eternity is unending.

**I have no greater joy than to hear that
my children walk in truth.
III JOHN 1:4**

CHAPTER V

Your Children

> " Behold, children are a heritage from the Lord, The
> fruit of the womb is a reward. Like arrows in the
> hand of a warrior, so are the children of one's youth.
> Happy is the man who has his quiver full of them. "

PSALM 127:3-5B

Our children hold a place in our hearts that no one else can fill. They are such an amazing blessing from the Lord. We see in Deuteronomy that He has commanded us to diligently teach *"Your children"* so it is obvious that it is our job. He does not leave it up to their Sunday school teachers or the public school down the street. He gives that command to us as their parents and He created families with a unique relationship of closeness and trust to help us do just that.

Train up a child in the way he should go, and when he is old he will not depart from it.
PROVERBS 22:6

This is homeschooling! Raising and training our children is our responsibility. What an awesome task God has entrusted us with. Homeschooling can be wonderful and exciting but it can also be difficult at times. We have high hopes and plans for what our days will be like but life can get in the way: kids get sick, the toilet overflows, someone knocks at the door etc. These things can be frustrating but they are part of real life and the way we react to these situations influences our kids. What kind of example are we setting? Are we teaching them to get angry and over react or to lean on God for patience and strength when things get crazy?

Another reason we can be overwhelmed with homeschooling is because at times, our kids don't have the best attitudes...and yes, we can admit that at times we don't have the best attitudes. I've been there, I know how difficult it can be to keep the right attitude when we are having a rough day. Attitudes are catchy, so if our attitude is rotten, chances are our kids' attitudes will start to become rotten as well, which will tend to escalate our bad mood and the cycle continues. If this persists, it can cause homeschool burn out and cause us to feel like quitting. The good news is-positive attitudes are also contagious. If we are joyful and pleasant, it will have an effect on our children's attitudes and homeschooling will be a lot more enjoyable.

> **A merry heart does good, like medicine.**
> **PROVERBS 17:22**

I do realize that our children can have terrible attitudes even when we continue to remain positive and calm; it can make for some long days. When we see this behavior become a pattern in our child, we should take extra time to pray for that child and look for reasons he or she may be struggling. Often, it goes deeper than just their moment of anger, crying, complaining or feeling overwhelmed. Obviously, we will need to correct their behavior but we should always be sensitive to how we do that. If they are outright disrespectful then that requires immediate consequences. Other times they may just need to take a break, get a quick snack, maybe get some one on one help with their work, or burn off some energy in the yard for a few minutes. There are other times when the issues go much deeper. When that is the case, we need to be patient with them and spend some quality time talking and praying with them. We should try to understand how they are feeling and be compassionate. Our kids deal with tough situations and feelings just as we do: issues with friends, hormones, lack of confidence, trouble dealing with change, worry, fear etc. Some kids readily open up about their feelings but others need some encouragement, they need to feel safe and know they can trust us before they will be willing to share what is in their heart. I have a close relationship with both of our daughters and give them each alone time to talk with me. They are completely opposite in this area. Ashlynn talks to me about anything and everything. I never have to wonder what she is thinking or how she feels because she is an open book. Aliya, on the other hand, keeps her deep or personal thoughts and feelings inside. She doesn't open up as easily but she knows she can trust me and when she is ready she will, with some prompting, let me know what is bothering her or how she is feeling. Our youngest guy, Liam, is pretty much in between. He doesn't mind opening up about how he feels if something is really bothering him but he sometimes needs me to ask questions to help him share his heart. Each child is unique; we must daily ask the Lord for wisdom to know how to meet their individual needs and share their burdens.

Bear one another's burdens,
and so fulfill the law of Christ.
GALATIANS 6:2

Sometimes our homeschool suffers because our children have lost respect for us or are disobedient. These are issues that will need to be resolved if we are going to have peaceful and productive days. We are responsible for how we raise our children. We want to be able to take pleasure in teaching, have joy-filled days and see them grow into the men and women God is calling them to be.

> Obey those who rule over you, and be submissive, for they watch for your souls, as those who must give an account. Let them do so with joy and not with grief, for that would be unprofitable for you.
> **HEBREWS 13:17**

> Children obey your parents in all things, for this is well pleasing to the Lord.
> **COLOSSIANS 3:20**

We must teach our children obedience and respect. The Bible commands children to obey their parents. Why? For this is well pleasing to the Lord. So we see that their obedience to us is not because we are so deserving or "because I said so, that's why!" but because it is obedience to God's command. We as parents need to help our children obey the Lord by teaching them to be obedient to us. Of course, we need to be sure that our expectations are reasonable and that when they are disobedient we correct them consistently and do so with love and grace. Disobedience and disrespect from our children can be frustrating and upsetting but we never want to discipline in anger, yell at them or degrade them. The Lord tells us in His word how we should treat others:

> Let all bitterness, wrath, anger, clamor, and evil speaking be put away from you with all malice. And be kind to one another, tenderhearted, for giving one another, even as God in Christ forgave you.
> **EPHESIANS 4:31-32**

It is easy to read these verses and forget that they not only apply to other adults but to our children as well. We tell our children how much we love them; yet are we treating them with love? Let's take a look at one of the most common passages on love in the whole Bible and relate it to how we treat our children. We typically think of marriage when we read it but it was written for all of our relationships in life, not just our marriage.

> Love is patient, love is kind, love does not envy; is not puffed up; does not behave rudely, does not seek its own, is not provoked, thinks no evil; does not rejoice in iniquity, but rejoices in the truth; bears all things, believes all things, hopes all things, endures all things. Love never fails.
> **I CORINTHIANS 13:4-8A**

Wow, what a standard of true love that is! When we evaluate the way we interact with our children we can ask ourselves, how closely we are following the instructions of these verses. If this is something we struggle with, and I'm sure we all do to some extent because we are human, we need to be willing to go to our children and sincerely say we are sorry when we mess up. Not only will we be setting a Godly example for them but we will also be strengthening the bond we have with them as they learn to trust us more. Just as I make them apologize to others, I have had to go to my children many times and apologize for the way I've spoken to or treated them. It has deepened our relationship because they know I am not holding them to a standard I am not willing to keep myself. God's commands apply to all of us equally and we need to do our best to live our lives for Him before our children. They are always watching us and learning from our example.

> **Do not provoke your children to wrath, but bring them up in the training and admonition of the Lord.**
> **EPHESIANS 6:4**

Now just because we are correcting them in love does not mean there will not be consequences. You reap what you sow and consequences are a part of the learning process. The reason for them is so they will remember and learn from their mistakes and will continue in the way they should go. Our goal is that they will have a heart change not just an outward obedience. We can have the most polite, respectful, obedient children but if their hearts are not changed by the power of God then what good will it do them? They may be well liked or more successful but those things only affect this life, we should, instead, be most focused on the next.

There are a few things we can do as parents to help our children become more obedient. Being consistent is huge! It lets our children know what to expect. When children know what is expected of them they are much less likely to test their limits. If they know you mean what you say they will question and argue less frequently. If you say something then mean it. Do not make threats that you are not willing and able to follow through on. As the saying goes, "Say what you mean and mean what you say but don't say it mean." Consistency is important in parenting and in homeschooling. If our children don't obey us in the little everyday things how can we expect them to be obedient in doing their schoolwork? How can we assume we will be able to teach them and raise them successfully if they are not willing to obey us? God's word is very clear that children are to be obedient to their parents.

> **Children obey your parents in the Lord for this is right.**
> **EPHESIANS 6:1**

Respect is another huge issue! We cannot let our children lose their respect for us at any cost. Once they do not respect us, it not only makes it difficult for us to get their respect back but it is also very hard to teach them anything. Respect is crucial for homeschooling successfully. Another concern is that once children lose their respect for their parents they soon lose respect for other adults and sometimes even for the Lord.

They often have trouble with authority, which can continue to be a detriment to them throughout the rest of their lives. Disrespect should not be tolerated and should come with a severe enough consequence that they understand the seriousness of it.

I let my children know why I require them to be respectful and obedient. I do it because I love them and I want it to go well with them. There is only one of the ten commandments that comes with a promise...

> **Children obey your parents in the Lord.**
> **"Honor your father and your mother," which is the first**
> **commandment with promise: "that it may be well with**
> **you and that you may live long on the earth."**
> **EPHESIANS 6:1-3**

Don't we want that for our kids...that the Lord will cause it to go well with them? No child is obedient all the time but if they are constantly being disobedient or disrespectful it is a reflection on our parenting and honestly, quite often partially our own fault. We can pray and ask the Lord to help us get back on track in our parenting. If we truly want it to "go well" with our children then we will teach them respect and obedience because we care about them. It also makes them a delight to be around. We will truly enjoy spending time with our kids, which is pretty vital since we are home with them all day.

Laziness is another major problem afflicting our children today. Because of our modern conveniences and self-centered society, kids have become self absorbed and entitled.

They expect the world to revolve around them and their wants. Years ago, children felt needed and useful knowing their hard work was a crucial part of their family's survival. Nowadays kids often sit on the couch playing on their phones, tablets or video games and complain when asked to do even basic chores. A lot of their behavior stems from the fact that we don't expect or require much of them. Our children, even at a young age, can be given chores to do and be held responsible for helping around the house. It makes them feel needed and shows them they are an important part of our family. We need to teach our kids to be diligent, cheerful workers, to look for ways to be helpful and to accept the challenge to do hard things. The rewards are worth it in the end.

> **The soul of the lazy man desires, and has nothing;**
> **but the soul of the diligent shall be made rich.**
> **PROVERBS 13:4**

Those of us who have more than one child understand the challenges we face helping our kids to get along with their siblings. We are all born with a sin nature, which makes us naturally selfish. Even as infants if you put two babies together with only one toy, they will fight over it. They do not think of the feelings of their playmate, they will have to be taught to be kind and thoughtful as they grow and mature. We can help our children become best friends with the siblings God has placed in their family by promoting togetherness as well as reminding them to think of others instead of themselves. When we put others first it strengthens the bond of love and friendship we already have with them. Having our kids pray for each other is another great way to encourage them to show love to one another. As homeschool moms we need to be sure we do not give our children reason to resent each other. Each of our children is unique and has their own strengths and weaknesses. When we compare them and say things like, "Why can't you be more like your sister?" or "Even your little brother knows how to do that, why can't you?" we are giving them reasons to be jealous and dislike each other. When they are unkind in the way they talk to or treat each other we should take the time to remind them what the Lord says about it.

> If someone says, "I love God," and hates his brother, he is a liar; for he who does not love his brother whom he has seen, how can he love God whom he has not seen? And this commandment we have from Him: that he who loves God must love his brother also.
> I JOHN 4:20-21

> Let nothing be done through selfish ambition or conceit, but in lowliness of mind let each esteem others better than himself. Let each of you look out not only for your own interests, but also for the interests of others.
> PHILIPPIANS 2:3-4

Our children are only little for a few fleeting years and then, before we know it, they are adults out on their own. Right now, we are the biggest influence in their lives. They look to us not only for their material needs but for almost everything else as well. We are the ones who hold them when they are sick, stop to look when they say, "Watch me!" for the millionth time and help them understand how the world works and how they fit into it. We have the chance to raise them with a Christian worldview, a strong faith, bold confidence and a firm foundation. As we continue to teach them to always turn to Jesus, as we walk the Christian life before them we are preparing them to meet the challenges of their future with the confidence that the Lord will always be there to guide them and to pick them up when they fall.

It is so critically important that we nurture the relationship we have with them now so that as they get older they will continue to feel comfortable coming to us because we have gained their trust. If we brush them off when they come to us with the little things when they are young, they won't come to us with the big stuff as they get older, because to them, it has all been big stuff. In our family, our children know that every night at bedtime they can talk to us about anything and we will always listen. Of course, they know they can talk to us any time of day but this gives them the specific opportunity to open up about how they feel or ask us questions without their siblings or the distractions of the day. We are trying to be intentional about establishing open and relaxed conversation with them as they are growing.

To really get to know each of our children personally, we need to take the time to look into their eyes when they talk to us and truly listen. It is so easy to be distracted by the seemingly important cares of this life that we let so many precious moments with our children pass us by. I feel like I have already missed so many moments because I was too "busy" to pause what I was doing and focus on my children. I am trying very hard to change that, to make an effort to be present in the moment and not distracted.

We have a tradition in our family that on the date of their birthday every month each child gets one on one time with me. For example, our son's birthday is October 17th so on the 17th of every month he gets his special time. Now of course life sometimes gets in the way and we have to do it on another day but it helps me to remember to take that time alone with them individually. We often just do something at home, like play a board game, bake or read books together. Other months I take them out for ice cream, go bowling or we go to a bookstore or coffee shop. The point is that I am building a relationship with them as the two of us talk and laugh together.

We are given this wonderful, yet short time together with our precious children. As we homeschool we need to be sure we are making a priority of leading them to Christ. Nothing is more important than the salvation of their souls. We should pray that the Lord will help us to take every opportunity we get to tell them of the great mercy of God, how He loved us so much that He sent His own Son to die for our sins. We need to remind them that the things of this world are passing away like a vapor, but what we do for the Lord lasts forever.

The world is passing away, and the lusts of it;
but he who does the will of God abides forever.
1 JOHN 2:17

There is nothing better than watching our children grow in grace and the knowledge of the Lord. Seeing them develop their own faith and their own personal relationship with the Lord is the biggest blessing any parent can ask for! I love watching my children worship during church or listening to them pray at bedtime or hearing them share the gospel with their friends. I am blessed when I see them choosing to spend time with the Lord. It is awesome to me to see a positive change in their attitudes, then have them tell me that it's because they've been praying about it and they know that the Lord is working in their life. Moments like these should encourage us to continue to steadfastly pray for them and bring them up in the way they should go.

Jesus said, "Let the little children come unto Me, and do not forbid them; for of such is the kingdom of heaven."
MATTHEW 19:14

CHAPTER VI

Sitting in Your House

Through wisdom a house is built, and by under-standing it is established; By knowledge the rooms are filled with all precious and pleasant things.

PROVERBS 24:3-4

I love being home. It's a place of comfort and love, a place where we can relax and be ourselves with the ones we love most. Our homes should be a peaceful haven, a place of shelter from the world. Being homeschooled, our children spend lots of time at home; consequently, the atmosphere of our home is extremely influential in their lives.

We, as moms, set the tone of our homes. Our attitude plays a huge role in our home and in our homeschool experience. If we are always tired, frustrated and angry, we can expect our kids to follow our example and our homes to be anything but peaceful. If however, we are rested and joyful, our homes will be a place filled with love and laughter and our children will be inspired to imitate our joy. Remember, more is caught than taught!

So how can we be joyful and rested when we have young children at home, schoolwork to grade, dinner to cook, an endless to do list and laundry that never ends? First of all, we can stop trying so hard and looking to ourselves, because in our own strength we will fail. We must always look to Jesus as our source. We can go to His word for wisdom and advice on how we should live.

Rejoice always, pray without ceasing. In everything give thanks; for this is the will of God in Christ Jesus for you.
I THESSALONIANS 5:16-18

> **Do all things without complaining and disputing**
> **so that you may become blameless and**
> **harmless children of God.**
> **PHILIPPIANS 2:14-15A**

> **Rejoice in the Lord always, and again I will say rejoice!**
> **PHILIPPIANS 4:4**

> **Be anxious for nothing, but in everything by prayer and**
> **supplication, with thanksgiving, let your requests be**
> **made known unto God, and the peace of God, which**
> **surpasses all understanding, will guard your hearts and**
> **minds through Christ Jesus.**
> **PHILIPPIANS 4:6-7**

The Lord in His wisdom knows that we are human and we have a tendency to get discouraged, tired, worry and complain. He was gracious enough to give us the answers to overcoming those things. Rejoice, give thanks, do not argue or complain, take everything to Him in prayer and let His peace, which truly passes all of our understanding, guard our hearts and our minds. He not only gives us the solution but when we ask He has promised to give us the ability to live it out.

Having a joyful heart can change our whole perspective. It isn't always easy; trials come in our lives, we can even get depressed but when we start to feel that way we can remind ourselves that:

> **The joy of the Lord is your strength.**
> **NEHEMIAH 8:10B**

So knowing this truth, let's remember to go directly to the Lord in prayer as soon as we start to feel down or overwhelmed and ask Him to give us His peace and His joy for our strength. When life starts to unravel, it can be so easy to turn to other things to try to make us feel better; social media, shopping, friends, food, even ourselves but He says to us:

> **Come unto *Me*, all you who labor and**
> **are heavy laden and I will give you rest.**
> **MATTHEW 11:28**

When we come to Him He will always be there to meet our needs. He is a faithful and unchanging Father. His mercies are new every morning. So remembering the goodness and mercy of God let's not only ask for His help but also spend some time worshiping and praising Him for Who He is even when we don't feel like it because He is always worthy of our praise. Put on the garment of praise for the spirit of heaviness. It will help take our focus off our problems and ourselves and put it back on how great He is and what He has done for us. Our victory has already been bought and paid for by His precious blood!

As we allow the Lord to change our attitudes, our kids will begin to enjoy learning so much more from their mom who is smiling and takes pleasure in teaching them. Our children are continuously watching us. If we are modeling the Christian life before them, they will take notice and will be attentive when we explain to them how it is that we can be joyful even on the bad days. We can point them to Jesus as we remind them that true joy is not dependent on our circumstances but comes from having Christ in our hearts.

> **Now may the God of hope fill you with all joy
> and peace in believing, that you may abound in hope
> by the power of the Holy Spirit.**
> **ROMANS 15:13**

It may not seem like it and may not be easy to do but getting up before our kids is a great way to start our day out rested and refreshed. Spending time alone with the Lord first thing sets our minds and our focus on Him; it helps us have the strength and patience we need to face the difficulties of the day. We don't have to go into our closet or kneel beside our bed to have that close personal encounter with the Lord, but we do want to set apart a time with as few distractions as possible. I will sometimes spend time kneeling before the Lord but other times I have my personal prayer time during my shower, while walking the dog or just lying in bed in the early morning while the house is still silent and calm. Other times I go into the family room, turn on some quiet instrumental music, and in the darkness spend time with my Lord before waking my kids to start our day. The point is not how or where we pray but giving the Lord priority, as well as our praise, and getting the refreshing we need from being in His presence.

> Truly my soul silently waits for God; From Him comes my
> salvation...My soul, wait silently for God alone,
> for my expectation is from Him. He only is my rock and
> my salvation; He is my defense; I shall not be moved.
> PSALM 62:1 & 5-6

> You will show me the path of life;
> in Your presence is fullness of joy;
> at Your right hand are pleasures forevermore.
> PSALM 16:11

When we pray we should ask God to give us His wisdom to help us be keepers of our homes. He has called us to this task and He can give us the understanding and grace to do it well by His power. We should ask Him to fill our homes with His love and with His Holy Spirit. When people enter our homes, they should notice something is different about them because the Lord is there.

As the keepers of our homes we are not only "keeping" it maintained in the physical but we are also to keep, or guard our homes by examining what we allow to go on in them. There are many definitions of the word "keep" in the Miriam-Webster Dictionary; two of those definitions are, "to watch over and defend" and "to refrain from granting, giving or allowing." Keeping our home means, we are protective of the things we allow to come into it. We need to be selective about what kind of music we play in our homes, the TV shows we watch, which friends we allow our children to have over too often etc. We must continue to pray that the Lord will open our eyes to anything that needs our attention and help us be willing to follow His prompting. When we are obedient to His voice, He will bless our homes with His presence, His peace, and with His joy unspeakable!

> **Admonish the young women to love their husbands,**
> **to love their children, to be discreet, chaste, _homemakers_,**
> **good, obedient to their own husbands,**
> **that the word of God may not be blasphemed.**
> **TITUS 2:4-5**

When we look at this verse, we can see that God commands us to be homemakers, but He also tells us to love and be obedient to our husbands. This may not seem like it has anything to do with our home, but in fact it does. A home where there is arguing and disrespect between husband and wife is not peaceful.

> **Every house divided against itself will not stand.**
> **MATTHEW 12:25B**

We can't control our husbands but we can, through the power of the Holy Spirit within us, control ourselves and how we respond. We can choose to show respect to our husbands even when we feel they don't deserve it, to love them unconditionally and to obey cheerfully. As we continue to do this, the Lord will bless us for our obedience to Him, our marriages will be stronger, and we will grow closer to each other than we ever thought possible. God's ways are always the best. Even in the busy years of parenting and homeschooling we need to be sure we are making time for our marriage. It can be easy to get so overwhelmed by the rest of our responsibilities that we allow our relationship with our husband to become neglected but taking time to be together is so important. We don't have to spend a bunch of money getting a babysitter and going out to a fancy dinner, although that can be fun occasionally. What we really need is to give our marriage daily attention. The little things can go a long way. We can stop what we are doing and look into our husband's eyes when he talks to us, surprise him with his favorite dessert, hold his hand when we are out and about or text him at work just to tell him how thankful we are for him and how much we love him. Our marriage relationships need to be cultivated so that they can grow and bloom into the close, lifelong love that God intends for us. Jordan and I have our kids go to bed two hours before us almost every night so that we can have time alone to talk, cuddle on the couch or spend time in our bedroom. Our children get an hour to read before lights out and they know that it is important for us to have time by ourselves. We are teaching them by our example that the marriage relationship should be valued and nurtured. Someday I pray they too will experience the love and closeness that comes from being married to your very best friend.

Let's not forget to daily pray for our husband and our marriage. God can do what we could never do. If our marriage is struggling He can restore it. He can bring back the love, joy and trust we may have lost. If our husband is not the kind of man we want him to be we can still be the wife the Lord has called us to be and trust Him to work in our husband's heart. Our children need a home where they know their parents love and respect each other. It not only makes our homes more peaceful but it gives them a sense of security.

If you are reading this as a single mom making this homeschool journey alone, remember that you are never alone. He has promised to never leave you or forsake you. He will come alongside you on your journey and give you the strength that you need. Don't forget to take time for yourself! You are filling the role of both parents and it can be easy to neglect yourself but you are important and you will be a happier, healthier mom for your kiddos because of it. So keep praying, keep trusting, keep loving and remember that even when we can't see it, He has a perfect plan for our lives. No matter where we find ourselves in life we can build a home for our kids based on love. Love makes our house a home.

We are building our homes, whether strong or weak, we are still constantly building. We do not want to build them alone, we want the Lord to be our architect and allow Him to help us build them for His glory.

> **Unless the Lord builds the house,**
> **they labor in vain who build it.**
> **PSALM 127:1A**

This makes me think of the story of the three little pigs. When we build our homes ourselves, in our own wisdom, we are building in vain using only wood, hay and straw. Our homes will not be strong enough to stand when our adversary, the devil, that wolf in sheep's clothing, comes against us. We will fail and our homes will blow away. However, when we allow the Lord to build our homes and look to Him for the insight we need, our homes will be strong and will be able to withstand his attacks. God is the master builder.

Jesus himself spoke another example of how we are to build our homes.

> Therefore, whoever hears these sayings of Mine, and does them, I will liken him to a wise man who built his house on the rock: and the rain descended, the floods came, and the winds blew and beat on that house; and it did not fall, for it was founded on the rock. But whoever hears these sayings of Mine, and does not do them, will be like a foolish man who built his house on the sand: and the rain descended, the floods came, and the winds blew and beat on the house; and it fell. And great was its fall.
> MATTHEW 7:24-27

What kind of foundation are we building on? Will our house be able to stand the storms of this life? Are we building our house on the rock? We may ask ourselves what/Who is the rock? Again, we can look to God's word for our answers.

> The Lord is my *rock* and my fortress and my deliverer;
> my God, my strength, in Whom I will trust.
> PSALM 18:2A

> For who is God, except the Lord? And who is a *rock*,
> except our God? It is God who arms me with strength,
> and makes my way perfect.
> PSALM 18:31-32

> For You are my rock and my fortress: therefore
> for Your name's sake, lead me and guide me.
> PSALM 31:3

From these verses, it is clear to see that the rock we need to build our homes, our lives and our families on is Jesus. He will be our strength. He will be our fortress from the storms of this life. Life is not always easy. Trials come in our lives and the devil is right there to try to use them to destroy our homes and our families. We may have marital issues, financial issues, health issues or relationship issues with family or friends etc. All of these trials come against us as raging storms but we are anchored to the Rock-our foundation is secure in Him. We are holding onto the one who commands even the wind and the sea and they obey Him. He may not deliver us from the storm or trial but He will be there in the midst of it just as he was for the three Hebrew children in the fiery furnace, just as He was for Jonah way down deep in the belly of a whale. He will be there with us through our storm. Even if things don't turn out the way we had hoped: divorce, loss of work, a bad report from the doctor, a death in our family, loss of friendships, He will stay with us all the way. He has promised to never leave us nor forsake us. Our homes may be shaken but they will not fall. They will remain firm on the Rock.

If it had not been the Lord who was on our side...then the waters would have overwhelmed us...then the swollen waters would have gone over our soul...
Our help is in the name of the Lord,
Who made heaven and earth.
PSALM 124:1, 4A, 5 & 8

"Fear Not, for I have redeemed you; I have called you by name; you are Mine. When you pass through the waters, I will be with you; and through the rivers, they shall not overflow you. When you walk through the fire, you shall not be burned, nor shall the flame scorch you. For I am the Lord your God.
ISAIAH 43:1B-3A

Praise God for His faithfulness to us even in the hard times! Just because we are going through hardships does not mean that we can't have peace in our hearts and our homes. The Lord can give us His peace that passes all understanding. We can trust in the Lord to work out our problems and we can, as He has commanded us, "Be anxious for nothing." Our kids look to us to lead them. If we are worried or fearful, they will sense it and be uneasy. If we are depressed and discouraged about life our homes will be lacking joy. If we are irritated or angry, we will be more easily frustrated and speak harshly or snap at our children, which will cause them to withdraw from us. If, however, we are keeping our eyes on Jesus as Peter did in the storm, we will find ourselves walking on water. Sure the waves are still there, He hasn't calmed our storm but He has calmed us right in the middle of it. Nothing that is going on around us will affect the peace and security we feel on the inside. With our home centered on Him, our family can rest having the assurance that He is in control and works all things together for our good.

> **The work of righteousness will be peace,**
> **and the effect of righteousness, quietness and assurance**
> **forever. My people will dwell in a peaceful habitation,**
> **in secure dwellings, and in quiet resting places,**
> **though hail comes down on the forest, and the city is**
> **brought low in humiliation.**
> **ISAIAH 32:17-19**

We see at the very beginning of this passage that there is a condition for our peace and that is righteousness, or "right living." Just like in the verse I referenced in the last paragraph, He works all things together for good "to those who love Him and are called according to His purpose." When we are living a life that is pleasing to the Lord, we will be at peace knowing there is nothing between our soul and the Savior. As that old hymn declares, "It is well with my soul." The effect that will have is a quiet, peaceful and secure home for us to dwell in. We also see in the last portion of this verse that the world around our peaceful and secure habitations can be anything but quiet, yet it will not influence us because our faith is not in this world. Our true home is in heaven.

> For we know that if our earthly house, this tent,
> is destroyed, we have a building from God,
> a house not made with hands, eternal in the heavens.
> **II CORINTHIANS 5:1**

Now that we have discussed our home's atmosphere and the part we play in building it let us look at our physical house. We do not need to have a big fancy house filled with top of the line matching furnishings; those things are nice but they won't last forever. They can not bring us true joy. It isn't about how nice our house is or the material possessions we have. It is about faith, family, unconditional love, laughing, playing and praying together. When Jesus is in the center of our lives, our marriage and our home then our children will know the pleasure of living in a home filled with His presence. Whether we live in a tiny apartment or in our custom-built dream house, we are the ones who make our house a place of comfort...a home.

Taking care of our home makes a difference as well. It is difficult to feel relaxed in a home that is dirty, disorderly or overly cluttered. Our homes need constant care and we are the ones called to be the keepers of them. Looking again at the word "keep" we can see another meaning through these additional definitions, "to take care of," "to maintain in a good, fitting or orderly condition" and "to have in control." Are we taking care of our homes? Are we in control of our homes? I am sure we all have areas in our home where we feel out of control. One of the areas I have trouble with is helping my kids keep their rooms clean. Like most kids in America today, they have way too much stuff, which can not only be overwhelming, but also causes them to be irresponsible in taking care of it all. Less is often more. We recently went through everything they owned and simplified. They really don't need lots of toys and piles of clothes to be happy. They are now able to enjoy their rooms and I will try my best to keep it from getting so out of hand in the future. I try to go through each room of our home a couple times a year and declutter. We accumulate so much in such a short time that it is necessary to re-evaluate what we have in our homes from time to time. Also, because we homeschool, we are home more than others are, so our homes get used a lot which tends to make them messy. It's easy for things to get out of control if we don't make a point of keeping up with them. Picking up as we go about our day and assigning daily chores for our kids (and ourselves) can be a big help. On the other hand, we don't want our homes to become an idol in our lives that cause us to neglect the time we have with our families or with the Lord because we are constantly worried about everything being in complete order. We need a balance. For some of us it comes naturally and for others of us it takes more effort. Every family has different priorities and standards to make their home feel comfortable for them. We aren't aiming for perfection or trying to meet someone else's expectations but rather just taking care of the home God has blessed us with.

The wise woman builds her house,
but the foolish pulls it down with her hands.
PROVERBS 14:1

She watches over the ways of her household,
and does not eat the bread of idleness.
PROVERBS 31:2

Even the way we decorate our homes can have an impact on our children. Everyone has different preferences and styles but simple things like displaying family pictures can give our children a sense of belonging and make our home feel like ours. We can also let our home speak God's word. His word is quick and powerful and brings life, so what better way to decorate and bring life to our home than with scripture? No matter what our decorating style, we can find art or wall décor with scripture to bring the truth of God's word into our homes. What a benefit it is to our children to see and read those verses every day. My husband's grandparents had a little sign hanging in their staircase with the scripture verse, "My God shall supply all my needs." They saw it every day, yet there came a certain day when their need was great and they did not know how it would be met, as his grandfather walked down those stairs that morning the Lord used that little verse of scripture to speak directly to his heart as a reminder of His promise. It was a blessing and an encouragement to him in his time of need. Praise God for His word! When we put thought into what we display in our homes and make the scriptures a priority not only will those verses be a reminder and an encouragement to us and to our children but their words will be imprinted on our hearts for years to come. His word does not return void.

> And these words which I command you today shall be in your heart...You shall write them on the doorposts of your house and on your gates.
> **DEUTERONOMY 6:6 & 9**

CHAPTER VII

Walking by the Way

 Then He went out again by the sea; and all the multitude came to Him, and He taught them.

MARK 2:13

Walking by the way speaks of our everyday life. Because we homeschool our children they are with us almost all of the time and they are constantly watching and learning. They most likely come along with us to the grocery store, bank, dentist, etc. Not only does this help them gain important life skills but they are also paying attention to how we treat others, how we react when things don't go our way, what we say and how we say it. These experiences are real world learning. Quite often, more education happens through everyday life than through their schoolbooks. These firsthand experiences will be remembered; they are practical applications in real life situations rather than fill in the blank quizzes. We have all probably heard the saying, "Tell me and I forget, show me and I may remember, involve me and I learn." How true. It's the reason why we have student teachers and intern doctors. The more we are involved in what we are learning the more we will retain the information and actually learn.

I love all of the memories I have of picnics in the woods discussing the plants, animals and God's love, the trips we took as a family visiting new places and learning about our country's history or all the times we spent just enjoying real life together. I learned so much more through those moments than through actual schooling. My mom even let my sister and I start our own "museum" from things we found on our many adventures. By the time we were teens it was actually quite impressive with everything from collections of shells, insects, foreign currency, rocks and minerals to random things like 5ft snake skins, porcupine quills, petrified wood, lava from a volcano we climbed in Oregon and an African elephant tooth.

It is amazing how many school subjects can be reinforced through life experiences. We can incorporate an impromptu science lesson while enjoying nature at a local garden, park or nature trail. We can discuss the types of plants, animals and insects we come across, what they do and why they are an important part of their ecosystem and the world God created. It's easy to find opportunities to point out things like pollination, life cycles, the food chain, the water cycle, disintegration etc. At home, we can talk about chemical reactions while baking or cleaning. There are times we can bring up how wonderfully the Lord created our bodies and give details about the different body systems. For instance when our children get sick we can explain the immune system or when they accomplish some goal we can remind them of the strength of the muscular system or the incredible brain that God has blessed them with and how it all works together.

> **I will praise You for I am fearfully and wonderfully made. Marvelous are your works, and that my soul knows very well.**
> **PSALM 139:14**

Math is often a subject that is disliked but we can use moments in our daily life to help them see an actual need to learn it because it is useful and necessary. Examples of this would be if we are helping to set up chairs at church we can use multiplication...6 chairs at each table and we have 8 tables so how many people can sit? Division: buying a pack of cookies for a snack and asking them to figure out how many each person will get. At the store they can use estimation to guess the total in the cart and see who is closest at checkout. (Don't forget to mention tax so they can work on percents.) And, if you actually still pay using cash they can figure out how much change you'll get back. Adding a tip to your bill when eating out is another good way to show how needed math is in life. We can work on fractions or ratios while baking together, keep track of time, mileage and directions while driving, use Roman numerals in telling time, measurements when sewing and on and on. Math is useful and needed and can actually be fun.

> **So teach us to number our days,**
> **that we may gain a heart of wisdom.**
> **PSALM 90:12**

History has come up during doctor's appointments. We have talked about Hippocrates and the Hippocratic Oath, Louis Pasteur, Clara Barton, Florence Nightingale, etc. We've talked about Thomas Edison when the power has gone out. During elections, we have discussed previous U.S. presidents, who they were, what they did and that several of them were homeschooled.

I sometimes even work on parts of speech with my kids while we are having fun. While we are driving, we will play "I spy a noun." At the park, we will practice having fun with verbs...

running, skipping, swinging, jumping etc. In the backyard, we work on prepositional phrases such as run *around the swingset* or swing *across the monkey* bars or hide *behind the tree* etc. When we are stuck in a waiting room, we play the adjective story game...I tell a story and every time I pause they give me an adjective to help me tell the story. It gets silly sometimes with beautiful pigs, a tiny princess, or purple monkeys.

More importantly, we can find many occasions in our day-to-day life to point our kids to Christ. If we are looking for them, we will find them. Of course, some moments are obvious and easy to take advantage of like talking to our kids about what they learned from their class at church or when our children specifically come to us and ask us about the Lord or our faith. Other opportunities come more subtly. We should pray the Lord helps us to recognize these moments and give us the right words to say at the right time. As we share with them, we don't want to be stiff, use rehearsed, boring words or give them the feeling they are being lectured, but rather it should flow naturally from our hearts and be genuine. Trust me, they will know the difference, and it will affect how they receive it. We want it to have a positive impact on their faith and their worldview.

Here a few examples of moments I have shared with my children:

When we are up early and share the beauty of a sunrise or in the evening as the red and orange glow of the sunset amazes us I have shared these verses...

The heavens declare the glory of God; and the firmament declares His handiwork. Day unto day utters speech, and night unto night reveals knowledge. There is no speech nor language where their voice is not heard.
PSALM 19:1-3

As we sit there gazing on the glory of God through the ever-changing sky, we discuss the great mercy of our God even to people who haven't heard the gospel yet; His very creation is daily revealing to them that He is real! It is declaring His glory. These verses were also a testimony to us the year we studied countries and cultures of the world. So many people don't have God's word in their native language, yet look how much the Lord cares about them by giving them His voice to hear through creation. What a merciful and loving God we serve!

Again, when we are out late and look up, we see through the darkness the stars shining in the nighttime sky, we remember how great and awesome He is!

He counts the number of the stars; He calls them all by name. Great is our Lord, and mighty in power; His understanding is infinite.
PSALM 147:4-5

> When I consider Your heavens, the work of Your fingers.
> The moon and the stars, which You have ordained,
> what is man that You are mindful of him, and the son of
> man that You visit him?
> **PSALM 8:3-4**

These moments may seem insignificant to us but in the light of eternity, we are encouraging our children to see this world through God colored lenses. We are helping them to stand in awe of Him, we are building up their faith.

Our kids absolutely love to be outside enjoying nature so we like visiting parks, gardens, bird sanctuaries or nature trails through the woods. I use these times to remind them of our God's great care for us and for all of His creation.

> Are not two sparrows sold for a copper coin?
> And not one of them falls to the ground apart from
> your Father's will. But the very hairs of your head are all
> numbered. Do not fear therefore; you are of more value
> than many sparrows.
> **MATTHEW 10:29-31**

It's great to have God's word hidden in our hearts so that we can easily share it with our children. Don't be discouraged if you not have memorized lots of verses yet because most of us have smart phones and there are lots of free Bible apps that can be downloaded. They have a search feature so you can look up verses related to whatever you are studying/doing. You can also use a Bible app when you know a portion of scripture that you would like to share but you don't have it put to memory yet. Here is a passage I have pulled out and read with my kids as we see God's creation around us.

Therefore I say to you, do not worry about your life, what you will eat or what you will drink; nor about your body, what you will put on. Is not life more than food and the body more than clothing? Look at the birds of the air, for they neither sow nor reap nor gather into barns; yet your heavenly Father feeds them. Are you not of more value than they? Which of you by worrying can add one cubit to his stature? So why do you worry about clothing? Consider the lilies of the field, how they grow: they neither toil nor spin; and yet I say to you that even Solomon in all his glory was not arrayed like one of these. Now if God so clothes the grass of the field, which today is, and tomorrow is thrown into the oven, will He not much more clothe you, O you of little faith? Therefore do not worry, saying, "what shall we eat?" or "what shall we drink?"or "What shall we wear?" For after all these things the Gentiles seek. For your heavenly Father knows that you need all these things. But seek first the kingdom of God and His righteousness, and all these things shall be added unto you. Therefore do not worry about tomorrow, for tomorrow will worry about its own things. Sufficient for the day is its own trouble.

MATTHEW 6:25-34

Wow, God takes such good care of His creation. It's sad how often we worry about the little things in life when we have such a compassionate God who has promised to meet all of our needs. We are human and we all get anxious from time to time. Our kids can become concerned about stuff too. They can worry about friends, schoolwork, their sports games, tests, death of loved ones, nightmares, sickness and the list goes on. At times, their fears can seem insignificant to us but to them these things are very real. We can remind them that even as adults we have the same stressful feelings. Our own worries can be over seemingly unimportant things that we know we shouldn't be nervous about or sometimes they are bigger things that seem impossible to us. No matter what the worry is, we can remind our kids (and ourselves) that God commands us to:

Be anxious for nothing, but in everything by prayer and supplication, with thanksgiving, let your requests be made known unto God; and the peace of God, which passes all understanding, will guard your hearts and minds through Christ Jesus.
PHILIPPIANS 4:6-7

I have shared with my children how God used this passage, which I had memorized years before, during a difficult time in my life. When Ashlynn was diagnosed with stage 3 cancer, I was, as most mamas would be, worried about what her future would hold and how we would get through this. I went to the Lord in prayer and He spoke to me through this verse. He simply said to me, "I said, 'Be anxious for NOTHING!'" I will be honest, my first response was, "But Lord, this is something big, my baby has cancer. This is something I have to worry about; I'm allowed to be worried about right?!" Again, He spoke to my heart, "I said, 'NOTHING' not 'Be anxious for nothing...but if it's really big, like cancer, than you can worry' I said NOTHING." As I sat there in that silent moment with God I could just imagine seeing Him on His throne, in all His glory, how big He is, how powerful He is. I knew someday when I was there in heaven I would look back and wonder why I even thought twice. There is nothing impossible for Him, there is nothing even difficult for Him. He is God Almighty and our problems do not take Him by surprise. I began to thank Him and praise Him for who He is, and as the end of that scripture says, His peace truly guarded our hearts and minds through the next years filled with tough decisions, hospital visits, treatments and scary unknowns. Later I noticed that the next verse gives us another practical application on how to be anxious for nothing.

> **Finally, brethren, whatever things are true, whatever things are noble, whatever things are just, whatever things are pure, whatever things are lovely, whatever things are of good report, if there be any virtue and if there is anything praiseworthy-meditate on these things.**
> **PHILIPPIANS 4:8**

We need to take everything to God in prayer, remember to thank Him, let His peace guard our hearts and our minds but we also need to guard and protect our thoughts. Keep our thoughts away from the negative and onto the pure, lovely and praiseworthy. No matter what we are going through, we can use the good or the bad to teach our kids to take it all to the Lord in prayer and stay focused on the good. He is always there for us and has His best for us even when we can't seem to see it.

> **And we know that all things work together**
> **for good to those who love God and**
> **are called according to His purpose.**
> **ROMANS 8:28**

Back to some more examples, I just get so excited about how good God is sometimes!

Going to the zoo is always fun no matter what age our children are. There are so many incredible creatures to learn about and as we discover more about them, they are pointing us to their Creator. We can clearly see His handiwork displayed in their uniqueness and remarkable abilities. It is evident that they had an intelligent designer and are not just the result of chance or some random explosion millions of years ago. God created this marvelous world to show us Himself. He, in His wisdom, created it all and all of it leads us back to Him. We can use trips like this to again remind them of what is truly important.

> But ask now the beasts, and they will teach you; and the birds of the air, and they will tell you; or speak to the earth, and it will teach you; and the fish of the sea will explain to you. Who among all these does not know that the hand of the Lord has done this, in whose hand is the life of every living thing and the breath of all mankind?
>
> **JOB 12:7-10**

A vacation to the beach can give us a visual way to show our kids just how much God loves them. His thoughts towards them are even more frequent than the grains of sand on the beach, even more than our own as their parents. It is comforting to know that as much as we love our children and want what is best for them, the Lord is even more loving and caring than we could ever be.

> How precious are Your thoughts to me, Oh God! How great is the sum of them! If I should count them, they would be more in number than the sand.
>
> **PSALM 139:17-18A**

A shopping trip can be a great time to remind our kids of what really matters, what has eternal significance. Sure, it's fun to get a new toy or outfit but those things don't last forever. Remind them how quickly they will get bored with that toy or how soon they will outgrow the new clothes. Our true joy does not come from the things we possess.

> Do not lay up for yourselves treasure on earth,
> where moth and rust destroys and where thieves break in
> and steal; but lay up for yourselves treasures in heaven,
> where neither moth nor rust destroys and where thieves
> do not break in and steal. For where your treasure is,
> there your heart will be also.
> MATTHEW 6:19-21

We can discuss that same verse when we make a trip to the bank. It is important to make wise choices with our money but we do not want to love money or put our trust in it because it does not last forever and it is not our source of happiness. As they get older and start earning their own money, we want them to have a firm foundation in financial decision-making. We can talk to them about generosity, tithing, saving, wise and foolish spending etc.

> For the love of money is a root of all kinds of evil, for
> which some have strayed from the faith
> in their greediness, and pierced themselves
> through with many sorrows.
> I TIMOTHY 6:10

> Remember the words of Jesus, that He said,
> "It is more blessed to give than to receive.
> ACTS 20:35B

> Bring all the tithes into the storehouse, that there may be food in my house, and try me now in this, says the Lord of hosts, "If I will not open for you the windows of heaven and pour out for you such a blessing that there will not be room enough to receive it.
> **MALACHI 3:10**

Sometimes our kids have disappointments because of delays or schedule changes. This can be hard, but it is a reality throughout our lives. My mom used to quote the following verse to us before giving us the disappointing news.

> Hope deferred makes the heart sick,
> but when the desire comes, it is a tree of life.
> **PROVERBS 13:12**

We always knew she was about to tell us something we did not want to hear but it was also a reminder that, as the verse says, it is an even bigger blessing when it does come.

When our kids fight and argue with one another, which is bound to happen from time to time, we can remind them of God's commands...

> Let all bitterness, wrath, anger, clamor,
> and evil speaking be put away from you, with all malice.
> And be kind to one another, tenderhearted,
> forgiving one another, even as God in Christ forgave you.
> **EPHESIANS 4:32**

If they are being lazy or complaining about their chores we can use God's word to correct their behavior in love.

> Whatever your hand finds to do, do it with your might.
> **ECCLESIASTES 9:10A**

> And whatever you do, do it heartily as to the Lord and not to men, knowing that from the Lord you will receive the reward of the inheritance; for you serve the Lord Christ. But he who does wrong will be repaid for what he has done, and there is no partiality.
> **COLOSSIANS 3:23-25**

> Do all things without complaining or disputing, that you may become blameless and harmless, children of God in the midst of a crooked and perverse generation, among whom you shine as lights in the world.
> **PHILIPPIANS 2:14-15**

Dealing with the pain of losing a loved one can be almost unbearable and watching our kids go through it is simply heartbreaking. Sometimes they are so young that they don't understand what is going on or grasp the reality of it. Our children are blessed to have had a close relationship with their great grandparents. We saw them three times a week in church and often stopped by their home to visit. I am so thankful for their Godly influence and the love they showed us. Just one day after Christmas in 2013, when our children were only 7, 6 and

4 years old, their "Great Papa" went home to be with Jesus. In the hospital, just minutes after Ashlynn found out that he had passed, she quoted to us the words of that old church song, "Well, someday soon, church I'm leaving…" then added, "troubles are over for Great Papa!" Just a few days later during his funeral, after doing nearly everything together and having been married for 66 years, their Great Grandma, in front of nearly 300 people, slumped in her chair and instantly joined her beloved husband with Jesus. Although we miss her dearly, it was honestly a beautiful thing to watch, she literally died of a broken heart. Talk about an emotional week for our young children! We had many talks about death and eternity. Being able to share scriptures with them about heaven and the hope we have of seeing our loved ones again was a comfort and a joy. Liam, having only just turned four at the time, started saying he wanted to die to go see them, so that was another opportunity to explain God's perfect plan for our lives and how we have to trust Him for our future.

> But I do not want you to be ignorant,
> brethren, concerning those who have fallen asleep,
> lest you sorrow as others who have no hope.
> For if we believe that Jesus died and rose again, even so
> God will bring with Him those who sleep in Jesus.
> **I THESSALONIANS 4:14-15**

And He showed me a pure river of water of life, clear as crystal, proceeding from the throne of God and of the Lamb. In the middle of its street, and on either side of the river, was the tree of life, which bore twelve fruits, each tree yielding its fruit every month. The leaves of the trees were for the healing of the nations. And there shall be no more curse, but the throne of God and of the Lamb shall be in it, and His servants shall serve Him. They shall see His face, and His name shall be on their foreheads. There shall be no more night there: they need no lamp nor light of the sun, for the Lord God gives them light. And they shall reign forever and ever.
REVELATION 22:1-5

To everything there is a season, a time for every purpose under heaven: a time to be born and a time to die.
ECCLESIASTES 3:1-2

These are just a few examples of times we used God's word to speak to our children's hearts. There are too many to list here but hopefully this helps us to see how our everyday lives point us to Jesus. Let's not forget to spend time with the Lord, hide His words in our hearts, pray our kids will be ready to listen and ask the Lord to give us the words to speak when these moments arise.

But sanctify (*set apart*) the Lord God in your hearts, and always be ready to give a defense to everyone who asks you a reason for the hope that is in you.
I PETER 3:15A

When Jesus was on this earth as a man, He was considered the greatest teacher to ever live. How did He teach? Did He buy the latest bestselling book from a popular Christian author to start a study group or buy textbooks and open a school? No. He did sometimes teach in the synagogues but most of His teaching was to people in the streets, down by the water or as they walked by the wayside. We also see Him using common circumstances to relate spiritual truths. Many of them were farmers, fishermen or shepherds so He used parables such as; the sower and the seed, the lost sheep, etc. He also used analogies that were relevant to them so they could easily understand: He is the vine we are the branches, I will make you fishers of men, we need only to have faith as a grain of mustard seed, He is the good shepherd and we are His sheep etc. They could relate to and comprehend these things with no trouble. We can do the same thing with our children; we can use the common and simple things to explain spiritual truths to them. There are so many Biblical examples found in our daily lives. Our children will remember these real life illustrations more easily than if they just read about them in a book because they are experiencing them for themselves.

I will give you just a few examples:

While we are driving, we can explain how we need to choose the right roads or we will never make it to our destination. The same thing is true in the spiritual sense.

> **Jesus said to Him, "I am the way, the truth, and the life. No one comes to the Father except through Me."**
> **JOHN 14:6**

> **Enter by the narrow gate; for wide is the gate and broad is the way that leads to destruction and there are many who go in by it. Because narrow is the gate and difficult is the way which leads to life, and there are few who find it.**
> **MATTHEW 7:13-14**

When we turn on a light in a dark, unfamiliar room, we can remind them that Jesus is the light of the world and without Him we will stumble and fall in the darkness.

> **Then Jesus spoke to them saying, "I am the light of the world. He who follows me shall not walk in darkness, but have the light of life."**
> **JOHN 8:12**

As we take care of our garden, we can show them that we reap what we sow and how that affects our garden/life. Taking care of a garden is a lot of work but in the end we get to enjoy the benefits of fresh produce. Our Christian life can be a lot of work but in the end it will be worth it all. Are we sowing to the Spirit or sowing to the flesh?

> **Do not be deceived, God is not mocked; whatever a man sows, that he will also reap. For he who sows to his flesh will of the flesh reap corruption, but he who sows to the Spirit will of the Spirit reap everlasting life.**
> **And let us not grow weary while doing good, for in due season we shall reap if we don't lose heart.**
> **GALATIANS 6:7-9**

As we walk by the way with our children let us take full advantage of the time we have with them. May we never miss an opportunity to point them to Christ and make an eternal impact on their hearts and lives.

CHAPTER VIII

From Rising Up Until Lying Down... and Then Some

To everything there is a season,
A time for every purpose under heaven.

ECCLESIASTES 3:1

Deuteronomy 6:6-7 pretty much sums up our lives as homeschoolers doesn't it? We are with our kids almost 24/7, walking by the way, sitting at home, getting up every morning and getting them to bed each night. Our job never seems to end. There is always something that needs to be done or someone who needs something from us. Schoolwork, housework, dinner, errands...how can we get it all done? Honestly, we will not always be able to but there are plenty things we can do to make getting it all done happen more often.

We can get so busy that it takes away from what really matters. When we are constantly running here and there we don't have time to enjoy life with our family, and in addition, it can cause tension, frustration and stress in our homes. The world says we need more to be happy...more possessions, more activities, more money when in fact Jesus is all we need. He is enough to satisfy! If we look to the things of this world to satisfy us we will never be content, because this world is not our home. We will forever be searching for that next best thing to make our lives complete when in reality the only thing that can do that is our relationship with Jesus.

> **Do not be conformed to this world, but be transformed by the renewing of your mind, that you may prove what is that good and acceptable and perfect will of God.**
> **ROMANS 12:2**

Let's take a good look at our calendars and see if there are things that can be simplified or eliminated. Many of us seem to be constantly busy. Not only are we busy with our own lives and activities but with our children's as well. There are more and more opportunities for homeschool kids these days than ever before. Co-ops, classes, field trips etc. not to mention sports! Socialization is something many homeschool moms worry about but we do not need to sign our kids up for every available program or activity. We foolishly believe that giving our kids more will prove our love to them or make them happy, but real joy can never come from activities or things. Don't get me wrong, giving our kids the opportunity to learn something new or fellowship with other children is great, but it must be done in moderation. When something starts controlling our lives whether it is our own schedule or our children's, we need to step back and make sure it is worth it. We need to evaluate the benefits and drawbacks of each activity, then learn to say no when needed. Our family should always come first. Kid's activities are fun. Helping at church or volunteering are great things to do but we need to make changes if these things begin dictating or adding stress to our lives. Some things are not optional, like doctor's appointments, shopping etc but if we plan ahead when scheduling these things we can save time, money and be at home more.

> **All things are lawful for me, but all things are not helpful.**
> **All things are lawful for me, but I will not be brought**
> **under the power of any.**
> **I CORINTHIANS 6:12**

Another consideration that is far more valuable than just our time are the influences on our children's lives. It is our duty as parents to protect our children; we want the majority of the influences in their lives to be Godly ones. Our children typically look up to adults in authority over them. Every coach, co-op leader, piano teacher, 4-H leader, etc. are all influencing our children in some way. Which way are they being pointed-towards Christ or away from Him? Many times, it's not just the adults but the kids they are around as well. We know their peers have a strong impact on them and can easily lead them astray so we must be careful who we allow them to spend their time with or become close friends with.

> **Do not be deceived: Evil company corrupts good habits.**
> **I CORINTHIANS 15:33**

> **He who walks with wise men will be wise, but the companion of fools will be destroyed.**
> **PROVERBS 13:20**

On the days that we are home, it really helps to have a routine to follow. Some moms do great with having a meticulous plan with specific times for everything. For most of us however, an extremely detailed schedule will lead to feelings of failure and frustration when things don't go as planned. We will get behind, then feel discouraged and irritated which can cause us to get angry or just give up. Having no schedule and just winging our school day can work for some families with self-motivated kids, but for most of us, half of our day will be gone before we know it and we will realize how little we have actually accomplished. Having no set plan can also cause more complaining and arguing from our less compliant kids when asked to get their work done. A routine however is not a strict schedule but rather an order to our school day. It helps our children know what to expect so that our days run more smoothly. In our homeschool we have a general start time and an order that our day follows.

We typically plan our routine together and write it out so that we can refer back to it whenever needed. Each year at the end of summer, we sit down and have a fun filled school meeting complete with freshly baked snacks and something tasty to drink. I let them voice their opinions on everything from curriculum choices to field trips or fun activities to helping come up with our daily and weekly routines for the year. It's honestly a lot of fun to hear their opinions and it lets them be involved with their education. I am showing them that I care about their ideas and desires. Of course, they know they can only offer suggestions; the final decisions are ultimately up to me. Sometimes they have very different thoughts on certain subjects. For example, Liam is an early riser so he always thinks we should start our school day early, this year he suggested 5:15am! Ashlynn loves her sleep so she thought that was a terrible idea and said 8:30am. Aliya thought her sister's time was kind of late since she is usually my most self motivated and prefers to get her work done earlier in the day so she came up with 7:30am. I listen to their opinions, write them all down in my notebook and then come up with a plan that works best for all four of us. Other times they say crazy things like, "No math for the year!" This last year, Liam, who was eight years old at the time and seriously always hungry or thinking about food, said he thought we should have a buffet. We all laughed at his silliness but when the first day of the new school year came around I had a surprise for them, they woke up to our entire kitchen table being set up as a breakfast buffet. It was a dream come true for him and his sisters were quite shocked and excited as well!

The one thing in our routine that stays unchanged each year is starting out our day with the Lord. Putting Him first and giving Him priority in our lives is one thing I have tried to instill into the hearts of my children from a very young age. We start each morning by seeking the Lord in prayer, reading His word and worshipping Him. For our worship time I have a playlist of praise and worship songs that we sing along with as we give Him the glory due His name. We also have several hymnals on hand so we can learn the old hymns of the church. This helps us keep our thoughts and hearts focused on Him. There is no better way to start our day out right. It is easy as homeschoolers to want to put our primary focus on academics, and of course, those are very important, but if we seek Him first He will help us get the rest done. Math doesn't last for eternity, science or history lessons won't matter in a thousand years, but time spent with the Lord has eternal value. A close relationship with their Savior and knowledge of His word will be far more valuable to our children throughout their lives than anything else we can teach them. Even if nothing else gets done, which hopefully isn't the case often, we can still look back at the end of the day and know that we put God first, that we took the time to speak His words into the hearts of our children and taught them how important their walk with Him is. We can rest knowing that we did not neglect the most significant part of their education.

Here is a little poem I learned as a teenager:

TIME TO PRAY
I got up early one morning
And rushed right into the day;
I had so much to accomplish
That I didn't have time to pray.
Problems just tumbled about me,
And heavier came each task.
"Why doesn't God help me?" I wondered.
He answered, "You didn't ask."
I wanted to see joy and beauty,
But the day toiled on, gray and bleak;
I wondered why God didn't show me.
He said, "But you didn't seek."
I tried to come into God's presence;
I used all my keys at the lock.
God gently and lovingly chided,
"My child, you didn't knock."
I woke up early this morning,
And paused before entering the day;
I had so much to accomplish
That I had to take time to pray.
Author unknown

> My voice You shall hear in the morning, O Lord;
> In the morning I will direct it to You, and I will look up.
> **PSALM 5:3**

If our children are close in age a great way to save time and encourage close relationships is to combine subjects whenever possible. Math and Language Arts will typically have to be done separately but you can find awesome curriculum that covers a wide age/grade range for most of the other subjects. Obviously when working together with several different aged children we should expect more from the older ones and less from the younger. Although sometimes the little ones will surprise us with how much they can grasp and retain, especially if they are trying to keep up with big brother or sister.

School is not the only thing vying for our attention. Our homes seem to constantly need to be picked up, swept, vacuumed, dusted (do people actually find time to dust?) not to mention the never ending dishes and laundry. If our children are still young, we should start teaching them now to clean up after themselves. This is something I did not do as well as I should have and I have paid the price for it by having to continually remind and retrain my kids. Since I have been a childcare provider for so many years, I have had many little ones in my home. When my own kids were young I had six children aged three and under at my house every day, so, although I did have them clean up their toys in the playroom, it was easier for me to clean up everything else during naptime than to have them come along side and help me. They are now much better at keeping up on their chores but we are still working on picking up after themselves without being told. All three of my kids have morning chores that must be done before breakfast and then they each have afternoon chores as well. The afternoon chores are bigger and we rotate them weekly so that they are learning to do all different kinds of housework. These chores must be done by the time Daddy gets home from work so that the house looks nice for him but they are also responsible for those specific chores any time they need to be done throughout the day. Every husband is different but it sure is more relaxing to come home to a picked up house, even just the areas where he will spend most of his time. It shows that we care. We should also make it a priority in our day to get anything done that he has asked us to do. Most guys would rather come home to find random things undone yet the one thing they asked of us done. When we make their wishes our top priority, we show them that we honor and respect them.

> Who can find a virtuous wife? For her worth is far above rubies. The heart of her husband safely trusts in her; so he will have no lack of gain. She does him good and not evil all the days of her life.
> **PROVERBS 31:10-12**

Schoolwork, housework, errands to run and then of course there is still dinner to be made....again...didn't we just cook last night? I actually really enjoy cooking but I hate looking up at the clock only to realize it is getting late and I have no plans for dinner. When I meal plan and shop for everything I will need, it is much less stressful. I know what I am making ahead of time so there is less last minute rushing around. We can consider what our week holds and how much time we will have each night and plan accordingly. When we realize we will be busy in the evening we can choose quick and easy meals, prepare ahead of time or use a crock-pot.

> She brings her food from afar. She also rises while it is still night, and provides food for her household.
> PROVERBS 31:14B-15A

Maybe getting it all done is harder for some of us because of physical illnesses or disabilities. Some of us may be dealing with other issues that hinder us from performing our duties to the best of our abilities such as depression or discouragement. All of these are very real factors that can make life more difficult but we know that the Lord can give us the strength we need.

> And He said to me, "My grace is sufficient for you, for My strength is made perfect in weakness." Therefore most gladly will I boast in my infirmities, that the power of Christ may rest upon me.
> II CORINTHIANS 12:9

Our weaknesses are actually an opportunity for the Lord to show us His mighty power. In our own strength, we will fail but in His strength, we can do all things. In the end, He will be the one who gets all the glory for what He has done.

We do have many responsibilities as homeschoolers, wives and mothers so we should daily pray for wisdom, patience and strength. The Lord has promised to give it to us when we ask. He will be with us and will help us to know what to do, or not to do, to serve Him and our families to the best of our abilities.

> If any of you lack wisdom, let him ask of God,
> who gives to all liberally and without reproach,
> and it will be given to him.
> **JAMES 1:5**

CHAPTER IX

Homschooling For Eternity

We do not look on the things which are seen, but at the things which are not seen. For the things which are seen are temporary, but the things which are not seen are eternal.

II CORINTHIANS 4:18

Eternity is forever, it is unending. With this truth at the forefront of our minds, how should we then spend our days? How should we teach? The few precious years we have with our children fly by so quickly, we need to make them count. The things we spend the most time on will have a strong influence on their lives. Are they things that will last forever? Will our children be able to look back on their homeschool days and be thankful for the firm foundation in Christ they were given?

Our children's hearts are like soil in which we are planting seeds. Whichever types of seeds we sow in them will grow in their lives. Are we sowing a love of achievement, recognition and success, a love of themselves and their desires or are we sowing a love of the Lord and the things that will last for all eternity?

> **For he who sows to his flesh will of the flesh reap corruption, but he who sows to the Spirit will of the Spirit reap everlasting life. And let us not grow weary while doing good, for in due season we shall reap if we do not lose heart.**
> **GALATIANS 6:8-9**

In verse nine, we see a reminder to, "not grow weary while doing good." The Lord knows that we will sometimes feel weary and want to give up, so He encourages us with the promise that we will reap if we stay faithful to our calling. At times, we can't see anything growing in their lives. Sometimes after putting so much time and love into our little heart gardens, the only thing we see growing are thorns and weeds. Our children talk back, are disobedient, fight, argue, treat each other unkindly, are selfish or rude and we start to wonder if anything we have taught them is actually taking root. We feel like we are failing. But even so, let us not grow weary, let us press on. Let us continue to plant, to water, to gently pull out those weeds and never stop praying that we will soon see our work come to fruition.

> **Those who sow in tears shall reap in joy.**
> **He who continually goes forth weeping, bearing seeds**
> **for sowing, shall doubtless come again with rejoicing,**
> **bringing his sheaves with him.**
> **PSALM 126:5-6**

When we sow literal seeds into the ground, we get back many more than we planted. One pumpkin seed will grow a vine with several pumpkins on it and they each have hundreds of seeds in them. One kernel of corn will grow a stalk with each ear of corn on it containing hundreds more kernels. The same is true of the spiritual; when we sow into our child's life we have no idea how far that seed will go. Maybe they will end up being a missionary or preacher who will bring hundreds of souls into the kingdom or maybe we will reap the benefit of watching them lead our grandchildren to the Lord. So, how much of a priority should we put on teaching them about God and His word? Well, how much fruit do we want to reap? I know I want to see my children grow. I want the garden of their hearts to bring forth abundantly.

> **He who sows sparingly will also reap sparingly, and he**
> **who sows bountifully will also reap bountifully.**
> **II CORINTHIANS 9:6**

We may be thinking that we don't want to be preaching to our kids all day long or constantly quoting scriptures. Of course, like anything, it can be taken to an extreme. Our motive should be to reach our children's hearts, not to show off how spiritual we are. We don't want our children to be self righteous because they know so many verses or Bible stories. If we are sowing the right seeds, with the correct purpose in mind and watering them always with prayer then the Lord will guard their hearts and minds. We should always strive to lift up Jesus, not our knowledge or our works. He is worthy and He will bring forth the fruit in their lives. So, what kind of fruit should we look for?

> **But the fruit of the Spirit is love, joy, peace, longsuffering, kindness, goodness, faithfulness, gentleness, self control.**
> **GALATIANS 5:22-23A**

As we take the time to pour God's word into our children's lives the Lord will quicken His words to their hearts. He will take the examples we live before them, the words that we say and use them to draw our children closer to Him. He is God alone. We cannot do it ourselves, we can only give what we have to Him and let Him use it. He is trustworthy and if He promised it, He will do it.

> **For as the rain comes down, and the snow from heaven, and do not return there, but water the earth, and make it bring forth and bud, that it may give seed to the sower and bread to the eater. So shall My word go**

> **forth from my mouth; it shall not return to Me void, but it shall accomplish what I please, and it shall prosper in the thing for which I sent it.**
> **ISAIAH 55:10-11**

Many people have suggested I put our children in public school and become a school teacher. This could sound like a good idea because I love children and I enjoy teaching. Recently the director of our local library tried to convince me to enroll my kids in school and be her children's librarian. As much as I know I would enjoy those jobs, they are not what the Lord has called me to do. I know I would never have true joy outside of God's will for my life, plus I would miss my kids terribly. I feel strongly called to be home, to raise my children and to love and support my husband. These may seem like unimportant jobs to some but to me they are the most important. I am touching lives. I am fulfilling my calling, through His power, and I have peace and joy knowing I am in the will of God.

> **Now may the God of peace who brought up Jesus from the dead, that great Shepherd of the sheep, through the blood of the everlasting covenant, make you complete in every good work to do His will, working in you what is pleasing in his sight, through Jesus Christ, to Whom be glory forever and ever. Amen.**
> **HEBREWS 13:20-21**

One day we will all stand before God and give an answer for how we lived our lives, what we did with the time He gave us. Did we follow His calling or did we go our own way? Was the time spent with our children used for Him? Did we raise them in His word and help to cultivate their relationship with Him?

For we must all appear before the judgment seat of Christ, that each one may receive the things done in the body, according to what he has done, whether good or bad.
II CORINTHIANS 5:10

What a heavy responsibility we have to raise our children in the way they should go. When our children accept Jesus as their personal Savior He becomes the foundation of their lives. When they are young we are daily building on that foundation. Let us carefully examine what kind of material we are using to build. Will it be strong enough to stand the test of time and hold up their lives? Are we building a foundation that will last into eternity? Of course as our children grow up they have a choice to make for themselves-to follow Christ or to reject Him. If we have an older child or children who have turned their hearts away from God and are choosing to live for themselves we can still continue to be an example to them, talk to them when opportunities arise and never cease to pray for them. Where there is life there is hope. Never give up, Jesus left the ninety-nine sheep to go after the one who had strayed, His love is that great! As I have said so many times throughout this book, may we daily seek the Lord for His wisdom and guidance as we endeavor to influence our children for eternity.

> For no other foundation can anyone lay than that which is laid, which is Jesus Christ. Now if anyone builds on this foundation with gold, silver, precious stones, wood, hay straw, each one's work will become clear; for the day will declare it, because it will be revealed by fire; for the fire will test each one's work, of what sort it is. If anyone's work which he has built on it endures, he will receive a reward. If anyone's work is burned, he will suffer loss; but he himself will be saved, yet so as through fire.
> **I CORINTHIANS 3:11-15**

I pray that this short, little book has encouraged you in your homeschool journey. I pray that the Lord will use it to touch your heart, that you will be reminded to keep Jesus first, look to Him for all of your needs and through you touch the hearts of your children. I love children and have always had a burden for their precious lives; your children were the motivating factor behind my writing. I have never written a book before and I am humbled to even think that the Lord could possibly use me in this way, but I must follow His leading. I am just a homeschool mom like the rest of you, trying to do my best to raise and teach my children. If the message of this book seems overwhelming to you, maybe there are many areas that you feel need to be changed in your home and homeschool, please don't feel defeated, change does not happen overnight. Pray and ask the Lord to show you something you can do to start homeschooling for eternity and then just focus on that one thing. Ask Him to help you and remember that when we mess up His mercies are new every morning!

I'm sure you can tell by now that I am passionate about homeschooling and about my faith. This book is just a minute sampling of the truths found in God's word. I pray you will continue to study it for yourself and apply it to your life and your homeschool. May you grow in grace and the knowledge of our Lord and Savior and may you continue to share with your children the truths that will last for eternity.

> Now may the God of all peace Himself sanctify you completely; and may your whole spirit, soul, and body be preserved blameless at the coming of our Lord Jesus Christ. He who called you is faithful, who also will do it. The grace of our Lord Jesus Christ be with you. Amen.
> I THESSALONIANS 5:23, 24 & 28

I would love to hear from you.

Email: joyforthejourney@protonmail.com

Mailing address:

P.O. Box 219

Jerry City, Oh 43437

Follow my facebook page:

Joy for the Journey-Erica Hunt

If this book has been a blessing to you please consider leaving me an honest review on Amazon.

A special thank you to...

My husband and very best friend, Jordan, for inspiring me and encouraging me every step of the way. I love you Babe!

My incredibly giving mom, who devoted so many years of her life to raising my sister and I in the way we should go. I am eternally grateful!

Karen DeBeus for graciously writing my forward. You have been a true blessing!

Miss Tina Mauldin and my wonderful mother-in-law, Karen, for helping me with my proofreading and editing. I am thankful to you both for all the time you invested.

Miss Durenda Wilson and Miss Tina Mauldin for being willing to write reviews for me. I sincerely appreciate you both and the kind words you had to say.

Marshall Cancilla, for patiently working with me to design and create my cover. You did an awesome job!

My friends and family for loving and supporting me through this new adventure. I am beyond blessed by each and everyone of you and thank God He has put so many amazing people in my life.

BOOK SUGGESTIONS

I love to read so I decided to give you a list of some of my favorite books. They have been a blessing in my life and I pray they will be a blessing to you as well.

Homeschool Books:

102 Top Picks for Homeschool Curriculum ~ *Cathy Duffy*

Big Book of Homeschool Ideas ~ *Debbie Pearl*

Called Home ~ *Karen DeBeus*

Educating the Wholehearted Child ~ *Clay & Sally Clarkson*

Real Homeschool ~ *Karen DeBeus*

Simply Homeschool ~ *Karen DeBeus*

Teaching from Rest ~ *Sarah Mackenzie*

The Unhurried Homeschool ~ *Durenda Wilson*

Parenting Books:

A Mom after God's Own Heart ~ *Elizabeth George*

Hands Free Mama ~ *Rachel Macy Stafford*

Instructing a Child's Heart ~ *Ted Tripp*

Jumping Ship ~ *Michael & Debbie Pearl*

Mom Enough ~ *Tony & Karalee Reinke*

Shepherding a Child's Heart ~ *Ted Tripp*

Six Ways to Keep the Good in Your Boy ~ *Dannah Gresh*

Six Ways to Keep the Little in Your Girl ~ *Dannah Gresh*

The 5 Love Languages of Children ~ *Gary Chapman*

The Life Giving Parent ~ *Clay & Sally Clarkson*

The Seasons of a Mother's Heart ~ *Sally Clarkson*

Books on Home:
A Home Full of Grace ~ *John & Susan Yates*
Home with a Heart ~ *Dr. James Dobson*
Home Warming ~ *Emilie Barnes*
Simple Secrets to a Beautiful Home ~ *Emilie Barnes*
The Life Giving Home ~ *Sally Clarkson*
The Life Giving Table ~ *Sally Clarkson*

Marriage Books:
100 Ways to Love Your Husband ~ *Lisa Jacobson*
A Wife After God's Own Heart ~ *Elizabeth George*
Created to be His Helpmeet ~ *Debbie Pearl*
The Love Dare ~ *Stephen and Alex Kendrick*
The 5 Love Languages ~ *Gary Chapman*
The Power of a Praying Wife ~ *Stormie Omartian*

**Curriculum I have used and
recommend for teaching multiple ages:**
Apologia Science (K-6th)
Jump-In (Apologia's writing program 6th-8th grade)
My Father's World Adventures in US History (1st-3rd) &
Exploring Countries and Cultures (3rd-8th)
Master Books Elementary Bible and English Grammar (4th-6th)
Mystery of History (K-12th)
Not Consumed Ministries Bible Study Guides (K-12th)
Winston Grammar (4th+)
Writeshop Primary and Junior (K-6th)